CULTURAL MAVERICKS

CULTURAL MAVERICKS

THE BUSINESS AND POLITICS OF INDEPENDENT BOOKSELLING IN CHINA

ZHENG LIU

Columbia University Press   *New York*

Columbia University Press
Publishers Since 1893
New York   Chichester, West Sussex
cup.columbia.edu
Copyright © 2026 Zheng Liu

All rights reserved

Library of Congress Cataloging-in-Publication Data
Names: Liu, Zheng (Sociology scholar) author
http://id.loc.gov/authorities/names/n2025026033
http://id.loc.gov/rwo/agents/n2025026033
Title: Cultural mavericks : the business and politics of independent bookselling in China / Zheng Liu.
Description: New York : Columbia University Press, 2026. | Includes bibliographical references and index.
Identifiers: LCCN 2025025845 | ISBN 9780231200127 hardback | ISBN 9780231200134 trade paperback | ISBN 9780231553452 epub | ISBN 9780231565011 (PDF)
Subjects: LCSH: Booksellers and bookselling—China | Independent bookstores—China
Classification: LCC Z462 .L59 2026 | DDC 381/.450020951—dc23/eng/20250616
LC record available at https://lccn.loc.gov/2025025845

GPSR Authorized Representative: Easy Access System Europe, Mustamäe tee 50, 10621 Tallinn, Estonia, gpsr.requests@easproject.com

To my parents

CONTENTS

Acknowledgments ix

Introduction 1

1 Book Publishing and Retailing in China 22
2 Searching for an Independent Identity 60
3 Culturally Adapted Strategies: The Concept 86
4 Implementing Culturally Adapted Strategies 115
5 The Economics of Independent Bookselling 157

Conclusion 209

Glossary 217
Notes 219
Bibliography 227
Index 233

ACKNOWLEDGMENTS

This book would not have been possible without the help and support of many people. First and foremost, I am deeply grateful to those individuals I interviewed for this study, who generously shared their time and professional expertise with me. Among them were bookstore owners, managers, shop floor staff, customers, book editors, publishers, wholesalers, authors, advertisers, journalists, book trade commentators, investors, and government officials. Their insights were invaluable to both my study and this book.

I would also like to extend my thanks to the many brilliant scholars and individuals with whom I engaged in thoughtful conversations throughout my research and writing processes. I am grateful to Angus Phillips, Zhiqiang Zhang, Hongyu Wang, Peter Williamson, Richard Owen, Julian Huppert, Ella McPherson, and Lavinia Harding-Rolls for their enthusiasm and support. My deepest gratitude goes to John Thompson, whose thoughtful guidance on my research and faith in my academic capabilities have shaped the kind of sociologist I have become. I am also immensely grateful to Laura J. Miller for her warm and encouraging responses to my emails. Her insightful advice gave me the confidence to pursue this project.

The journey to completing this book was a long one, during which a global pandemic took place, and I moved institutions and cities to take up a new job. I would never have been able to finish this book without the unwavering support of Columbia University Press. I owe a debt of gratitude to Eric Schwartz, now director of New York University Press, whose patience, understanding, and faith in this book were vital to its completion. I am also very grateful to Lowell Frye and Alyssa Marie Napier for their outstanding coordination of this project from start to finish.

Finally, I dedicate this book unreservedly to my parents, who have always been my ultimate source of strength, faith, and curiosity in life. Their love and support have sustained me throughout this journey, and for that, I am forever grateful.

CULTURAL MAVERICKS

INTRODUCTION

Starting from the mid- to late 2000s, a collection of bookstores claiming to be "independent" began to appear across China. Initially concentrated in large cities, these establishments gradually started to appear in smaller cities as well. Throughout the 2010s, the number of these independent bookstores continued to grow, and their influence was increasingly felt both within and beyond the bookselling field. Their stories began to be told by trade observers at major book industry conferences, triggering much interest in them from fellow booksellers, publishers, editors, authors, advertisers, and others. Regular bookstore customers would often learn about this new species of bookstore through extensive media stories about these characterful establishments.

This rapid rise of independent bookstores, however, took place against a backdrop that made it a phenomenon not only unexpected but also, in a sense, counterintuitive. During the 2000s, under the dual pressures of competition from online bookstores and other digital transformations in the wider book industry, many brick-and-mortar bookstores in China permanently closed their doors. This widespread closure of traditional physical bookstores made the concurrent proliferation of independent bookstores an interesting and important phenomenon to study: It offers a valuable lens through which to better understand both the changing book culture in China in the digital age and the unique yet evolving dynamics of cultural production and consumption in this country.

So what are the driving forces behind the emergence and development of independent bookstores? How are these bookstores different from the *nonindependent* bookstores that have long existed in the Chinese bookselling field? What unique values do independent bookstores create for customers that afford them a competitive advantage in the highly competitive business of book retailing? What strategies do independent bookstores employ to create, deliver, and capture such values? And finally, what impact does the rise of independent bookstores have on the evolving book culture and dynamics of cultural production and consumption in China in the twenty-first century?

To answer these questions, I embarked on a decade-long investigation into these organizations, hoping to unveil both their secrets to business success and the broader social, cultural, political, and technological conditions that underpinned this success. To do so, I spoke with over one hundred book industry practitioners, including sixty-three formal interviews with owners or managers of independent bookstores; I visited numerous bookshops, both independent and nonindependent, and talked to many bookstore customers; I joined a social media group for independent booksellers and followed their conversations and discussions for over a decade; and finally, I gathered and analyzed hundreds of media stories, trade reports, government policy documents, business analyses, bookstore marketing materials, and other documents. Since the study began in 2014, enough time has passed that the world of independent bookselling has changed further in certain aspects. Some of the independent bookstores I studied closed down, but time, in this instance, was not my enemy. On the contrary, it has done an important service to this book by allowing me to test my findings and arguments against some recent developments in independent bookselling. This exercise showed that my conclusions not only remain valid but also possess a transferable explanatory power in illuminating not just the emergence but also the evolution of independent bookselling in China.

APPROACHING INDEPENDENT BOOKSTORES

My journey to study independent bookstores was not a smooth one. Two challenges I encountered have shaped my approach to and final understanding of them.

The first challenge I encountered was to define "independent bookstore" in the Chinese context. Without a clear and effective definition of this concept and its designated object, I could not even identify the proper research subject for my study. The challenge, however, was that when I first started my research, the term "independent bookstore"—*duli shudian* in Chinese—was still too new a concept in the Chinese book trade to have a settled and commonly agreed definition, even among those who were actively using it. That is, unlike in the Western book industry, where "independent bookstore" is a well-established notion referring to bookshops owned and run by individual or noncorporate proprietors, in the Chinese book business in 2014, there existed no fixed or commonly agreed opinion on the features and attributes that would make a bookstore independent. This ambiguity presented a challenge: I had to find a way to study something without fully knowing what it was. As a result, investigating how the concept of "independent bookstore" was understood, defined, and used by Chinese book industry practitioners to designate a distinct new type of bookstore became my first research question.

While chapter 2 will provide a detailed analysis of this concept, it is useful to briefly outline it here to give the reader a better understanding of the research object and central theme of this book. Put succinctly, this book examines a group of bookstores that refer to themselves as independent to differentiate themselves from the two major types of physical bookstores in the Chinese bookselling field: the state-owned Xinhua Bookstore, on the one hand, and the regular, nonindependent, privately owned bookstores, on the other. Independent bookstores differ from the state-owned Xinhua Bookstore for being owned and run by private, i.e., nonstate, proprietors, whereas they distinguish themselves from other privately owned bookstore through a stronger emphasis on cultural sophistication and moral commitment.

It is important to note that the title "independent bookstore" is a self-appointed one. This means that, in theory, any bookstore can claim to be an independent bookstore, or *duli shudian*, without requiring external validation. In practice, however, bookstores adopting this label tend to operate within a shared understanding of its meaning and scope and apply a set of criteria to evaluate their independent status. Not being owned by the state is universally accepted as the single most important signifier of independent identity in the Chinese context, but two other factors are also significant. First, an independent bookstore must have operational autonomy. Although debates exist over whether such autonomy necessitates individual ownership (hence, excluding corporate-owned bookstores) and a single-store operational mode (as opposed to a chain operation), all of the self-identified independent booksellers I interviewed agreed that the ability to manage the store's core business activities, particularly book selection, without having to obey an external party's instruction is an essential quality of a *duli shudian*. Second, most interviewees also emphasize individuality (*gexing*) as a key marker of independence and link it to nonconformity, which describes an ability to offer alternative perspectives and maintain intellectual autonomy.

At the same time, these bookstores also differ from their Western counterparts. Notably, the two defining features of independent bookstores in the United States and the United Kingdom—being nonchain-owned and locally oriented—are simply irrelevant to how Chinese independent booksellers perceive their independent identity. The way in which they instead conceive of and articulate their independent identity will be discussed in detail in chapter 2.

The second challenge I encountered was the scarcity of academic literature on the Chinese book business, especially literature that examines the relationship between developments in this sector and broader sociocultural trends in China from a sociological perspective. Paradoxically, despite being the oldest and most established segment of the wider media and cultural industry, the book business—including book publishing and bookselling—has received surprisingly little attention from scholars studying the intersections of media, culture, and society. This stands in stark contrast to the extensive literature on the production, distribution, and consumption of other media products, such as newspapers, magazines, television, social media, and the internet. As a result, research on the social organization, processes, and consequences of book publishing and bookselling remains both scanty and relatively peripheral in the social study of media and culture. It concentrates mainly on two specialist fields of study: publishing studies, on the one hand, and the cultural sociology of the book, on the other. It is within these two bodies of literature that this study is grounded.

Publishing studies is a specialized subfield of literary studies concerned with understanding the organizational, operational, and processual dimensions of the publishing industry, including bookselling. As an interdisciplinary field of study, publishing studies caters to both academic and professional audiences interested in understanding and theorizing the dynamics of the publishing business. In addition to its interdisciplinarity, publishing studies is highly international in scope. *Logos: Journal of the World Publishing Community* and *Publishing Research Quarterly*, the two leading academic journals in this field, have both published extensive research on publishing and bookselling in non-English-speaking contexts, including China. The rich material on the Chinese book industry published by these two outlets has been instrumental to my research. Moreover, my research also drew upon and benefited from a collection of research monographs written by publishing studies scholars and publishing industry practitioners, among which Giles Clark and Angus Phillips's *Inside Book Publishing*, Robert Baensch's *The Publishing Industry in China*, and Guangwei Xin's *Publishing in China* were the most important texts.[1]

Alongside publishing studies literature, this study is built on and expands a body of literature that examines the book business and book culture from a sociological perspective. Within this space, Laura J. Miller's *Reluctant Capitalists* (2006) and John B. Thompson's *Merchants of Culture* (2010) are particularly influential in shaping this study.[2]

Focusing on book retailing, Miller explores how the evolution of America's bookselling industry during the twentieth century both shaped and was shaped by the country's evolving consumer culture. Her meticulously researched and beautifully written book demonstrates that the ups and downs experienced by America's independent bookstores during this period were not isolated events. Rather, they reflected a broader cultural and economic transformation in American society: the rise and dominance of commercialism in the cultural sector and the accompanying struggles and resistance from cultural producers like independent booksellers. Miller's work demonstrates how studying developments in the book business by situating the analysis within the broader context of social, cultural, and economic transformations can deepen our understanding of both subjects. Thompson's work investigates the social structure of trade book publishing in the English-speaking world in the twenty-first century. As he describes it, the study aims to "lay bare the fundamental dynamic that has shaped the evolution of this field over the last few decades and, on the basis of this analysis, to offer a critical reflection on the consequences of these developments for our literary and intellectual culture."[3] That is, like Miller's work, Thompson's study also seeks to demonstrate how developments in the book business tend to coevolve with—that is, shape and be shaped by—cultural, economic, societal, and technological shifts in the wider society. This distinctive sociological perspective—the standpoint that developments in the book business cannot be fully understood without considering their relationships with broader social, cultural, economic, and technological transformations—is a key epistemological stance that also underlies my approach to understanding the rise of independent bookstores in China.

Another key contribution of Miller's and Thompson's works is that they highlight the importance of examining the economic dimensions of booksellers and publishers—for example, their need to attract customers, win competition, make a profit, expand their business, satisfy investors, repay debts, and so on—to understanding their motives and actions. In the book industry, independent bookstores are particularly prone to romanticization; owners and workers are frequently portrayed in popular discourse as noble guardians of cultural values in the face of commercialism, with little regard for the monetary returns of their business. This narrative has also affected perceptions of independent bookstores in China. Much of the existing media coverage and trade analysis of these bookstores overemphasizes their cultural motivations and commitments while overlooking their economic drives. As such, one of the goals of this book is to rectify this issue and show how economic considerations have driven and shaped the development and practices of independent bookstores.

THEORETICAL PERSPECTIVES

Answering the questions asked at the beginning of this introduction requires delineating several core concepts and relationships. Most important, it involves the clarification of two key sets of perspectives.

Bookselling Culture

First, independent bookstores should be understood as both cultural institutions and cultural enterprises. As cultural institutions, a core aspect of their independent identity is how these bookstores view their roles in distinctive cultural terms. They perceive themselves as crucial purveyors of culture in society, especially high culture, which is defined in this context as a cultural approach that prioritizes artistic and intellectual values over economic and political ones in the creation, distribution, and consumption of cultural goods. This cultural orientation disposes the actions of independent bookstores and shapes all major aspects of their business activities. Seeing independent bookstores as cultural institutions is therefore crucial for understanding their development and practices.

On the other hand, the label "cultural enterprise" highlights the economic nature of independent bookstores, which are inherently for-profit business entities operating in a fiercely competitive, market-driven industry. In their daily operations, independent bookstores interact with a wide range of market players—publishers, wholesalers, rival booksellers, investors, marketeers, advertisers, and others—and are influenced by the decisions and actions of these actors. Meanwhile, as participants in the broader economic sphere, independent bookstores are subject to the overarching rules and logics governing this domain. As a result, economic imperatives, such as survival, competition, collaboration, profitability, growth, efficiency, and innovation, are just as important in shaping the behavior and activities of independent bookstores as their cultural orientation. A critical analysis of independent bookstores must consider the impact of economic factors.

Understanding independent bookstores as both cultural institutions and cultural enterprises underpins my analysis in this book. To do so, I introduce the concept of "culturally adapted strategy" to illustrate how these bookstores navigate and pursue both their cultural and economic goals. Three such strategies, namely political framing, moral positioning, and cultural distinguishing, are employed.

Political framing involves presenting a bookstore's activities (e.g., book selection, events) in political terms, either explicitly or implicitly, to create a distinct identity. Most bookstores adopting this strategy do so to position themselves as alternatives to mainstream bookstores in the market—both state-owned Xinhua Bookstores and commercially driven privately owned bookstores—by accentuating their commitment to fostering spaces for the free exchange of diverse ideas. A small number of bookstores go further by directly but discreetly challenging state influence in the book industry by, for instance, promoting politically sensitive titles or hosting controversial authors for events. The strategy of political framing, therefore, serves a dual function in China's independent bookstores: It enables these bookstores to achieve their critical economic goal of differentiating themselves from competitors in the market while also providing those politically minded bookstore owners with a means to embed and express their personal sociopolitical views through bookselling.

Moral positioning describes the processes in which independent bookstores give moral meanings to their activities and present themselves as morally concerned to differentiate themselves from other types of bookstores in the market. Bookstores adopting this strategy, for example, have been seen to refuse to engage in aggressive price-cutting (which is common among online retailers), asserting that selling books at fair prices respects authors' and editors' intellectual labor and helps preserve the integrity and order of the book publishing and retailing industries.

Finally, the strategy of cultural distinguishing enables independent bookstores to attract affluent, distinction-seeking customers by offering them unique and sophisticated cultural experiences. Bookstores adopting this strategy differentiate themselves by curating refined book collections, creating stylish store environments, and hosting diverse cultural events, such as poetry readings, tea tastings, and art exhibitions. Drawing on Thorstein Veblen, I argue that visiting independent bookstores constitutes a form of conspicuous consumption, where customers willingly pay a premium for a culturally enriching experience that signals their refined cultural taste and elevated social status.[4] Cultural distinguishing thus allows independent bookstores to harness this growing market of affluent, distinction-seeking consumers to achieve their economic goal of surviving and thriving in the highly competitive bookselling industry.

While these culturally adapted strategies enable independent bookstores to pursue both cultural and economic goals, their development is nevertheless driven primarily by the bookstores' cultural aspirations, most notably their shared belief that culture, rather than any other forces, should play a central and autonomous role in the field of cultural production. The culturally adapted strategies thus manifest independent bookstores' deep-seated desire to reassert culture's central and autonomous role in the Chinese cultural production field, of which bookselling constitutes an important part. Specifically, the strategy of political framing stems from the bookstores' concern about the influence of political power in cultural production, and the strategies of moral positioning and cultural distinguishing address their apprehensions about the rising power and growing dominance of commercialism in book retailing. Together, these three culturally adapted strategies represent and constitute independent bookstores' collective efforts to reinstate culture's leading role in the Chinese cultural field by actively grappling with the forces they perceive as undermining it.

However, whichever of these strategies an independent bookstore might employ, their goal is to cultivate a niche market in which they are seen by customers as both different from and more attractive than their competitors. That is, in addition to helping independent bookstores to recentralize and reprioritize cultural rules and values in book retailing, these culturally adapted strategies help create a unique appeal for customers that distinguishes an independent bookstore from its competitors and lets it stand out in the highly competitive market of bookselling. Indeed, as new entrants in this demanding industry, independent bookstores must develop a competitive advantage in order to survive. The three culturally adapted strategies effectively serve this purpose by enabling these bookstores to generate values for customers that are not only unique and attractive but also difficult for competitors to replicate. This ability to create and deliver niche value is the key to the survival and success of independent bookstores.

Bookselling and Chinese Culture

Second, it is crucial to understand the development and practices of independent bookstores within the broader context of the interactions among cultural, political, and economic forces and processes shaping the Chinese cultural sphere. The existing English-language literature on Chinese media and cultural production has a long-established tradition of analyzing developments in these sectors through the lens of state-society and state-market struggles.[5] In this tradition, nonstate-owned players in the media and cultural industries are frequently characterized as politically and ideologically driven to contest with state-owned actors and their perspectives. A distinctive resistance narrative is therefore in place in this literature for analyzing the cultural politics—that is, the political motivation and influence—of nonstate-owned media and cultural participants in China. Within this framework, these nonstate actors are sometimes referred to as "independent," a label highlighting that their access to nonstate financing facilitates their operational autonomy from state jurisdiction.[6]

I began this study influenced by this approach, hypothesizing that a key driving force behind those unconventional, privately owned *independent* bookstores was an intention to create political or ideological effects, such as challenging mainstream narratives in the Chinese cultural and intellectual spheres by selling controversial books or hosting events with controversial speakers. The empirical data I collected, however, did not support this hypothesis. Instead, they show that independent bookstores are far less politically concerned than some actors in certain other media and cultural fields, such as journalism. Hardly any independent bookstore owners I interviewed entered the business with the aim of fulfilling a political objective.

But does this mean that political factors are irrelevant to understanding independent bookstores? Not necessarily. In my opinion, the interplay between cultural, political, and economic forces and processes remains crucial in shaping the development and practices of independent bookstores. What differentiates my findings from previous studies is that the dynamics of their interactions are far more nuanced than otherwise suggested. For example, I found that cultural and economic goals play a decisively more important and direct role in affecting independent bookstores' decision-making than political considerations. While concerns about political influence in the book business were widespread among the independent booksellers I interviewed, such concerns were more prominent in their general reflections on the industry's status quo and less directly relevant to the daily operations of their bookstores. Instead, political considerations tend to come into play only when doing so is considered conducive to the bookstores' pursuit of cultural and economic goals. For instance, although there were instances where independent bookstore owners sold controversial books as a way of expressing their personal political viewpoints, most of the independent bookstores I studied employed the strategy of political framing to differentiate themselves from their competitors and better attract customers. Similarly, although all the independent booksellers I interviewed considered nonstate ownership a core criterion of the independent identity, as discussed earlier, their distancing from the state is driven by their desire to preserve their economic and cultural autonomy, not out of any intrinsic antagonism toward the state.

METHODOLOGICAL APPROACH

This book draws on data collected from a wide range of sources from 2014 to 2023, using several qualitative research methods. Qualitative methods were selected because they aligned better with the study's aim of understanding the rise of independent bookstores by examining the lived experiences and perspectives of individual independent booksellers. Unlike quantitative methods, which are more suited to testing existing theories using numerical data, qualitative methods focus on generating theory through the interpretation of narrative data.[7]

Three qualitative research methods were employed to collect data: semistructured, in-depth interviews, observation, and documentary analysis. Semistructured, in-depth interviews allow researchers to interpret the actions and social contexts of their research objects from the participants' own perspectives.[8] I decided that interviews were the most suitable tool for achieving the goal of comprehending the decisions and actions of independent bookstores through their own voices, and I made this my primary method for data collection. During three sets of fieldwork in China—between late 2014 and mid-2015, in early 2017, and in early 2019—I visited and studied a total of fifty-nine independent bookstores across six Chinese cities. All of these bookstores self-identified as independent bookstores (*duli shudian*). Bookstores of varied sizes—ranging from small, individually owned shops to larger, corporation-run stores—were selected to ensure a representative sample of the sector. Data were collected through sixty-seven formal, recorded interviews with bookstore owners, managers, and other key personnel, as well as with three publishers and one government official. Additionally, I had many informal conversations with operators of nonindependent bookstores, editors, wholesalers, authors, journalists, advertisers, and book trade analysts, as well as with over two dozen bookstore customers whom I encountered during my visits to the bookstores.

As is common in interview-based qualitative research, participant recruitment for this study began with "cold" contacting. Before my first fieldtrip, I compiled a list of independent bookstores I particularly wanted to visit and made initial contact with some of them. However, in most cases, I adopted a more direct approach by simply visiting the bookstore in person, introducing myself, and politely asking if I could speak with the owner or manager about an academic study of independent bookstores. This method proved highly successful, resulting in interviews with nearly all the bookstores I approached. In the few cases where this method was less effective, I employed snowball sampling to recruit the target participants. Nevertheless, the vast majority of interviews were secured through direct, in-person contact.

Most interviews with booksellers were conducted onsite at their bookstores, and those with publishers, editors, and other individuals took place either in their offices or in coffee shops. Each participant was provided with an oral introduction to the study and a printed informed consent form outlining key details, such as the right to withdraw, recording arrangements, anonymity options, data confidentiality, and data usage plans. The interviews varied in length, ranging from under an hour to four hours, with the majority lasting between 90 and 180 minutes. For those informal conversations, participants were similarly informed about the study's purpose and data usage plans. All interviews were recorded using a digital recorder, and I later transcribed them. In cases where recording was not possible, extensive notes were taken to document the discussions. All transcripts and field notes were imported into the qualitative data analysis software program MAXQDA for coding and thematic analysis.

In addition to interviews, I conducted over two hundred hours of extensive observation in bookstores. During each visit, I meticulously documented how books were arranged and displayed, the design and decor of the shop, and the range of products and services offered. This effort resulted in over two hundred photographs and more than sixty thousand words of fieldnotes. I also attended over thirty events hosted by independent bookstores and took detailed notes on each. Apart from independent bookstores, I conducted observations in more than twenty-five nonindependent bookstores and six book wholesale centers. I also attended the 2015 and 2017 Beijing Book Fairs, where I participated in several trade conferences. Since 2015, I have been a member of a WeChat group for independent booksellers, where I have continuously observed and analyzed discussions and debates within this virtual community. This participation has provided me with ongoing insights into the evolution of independent bookselling during my time away from China. For example, the group's membership grew from under one hundred in 2015 to nearly five hundred by early 2023, an indication of the steady growth of the field over the years. Finally, I consulted a wide range of documentary materials, including trade reports, government policy documents, official statistics, company financial reports, media reports, social media articles, and bookstore marketing materials. These materials were not only essential for data triangulation but also served as valuable datasets in their own right.

MAIN ARGUMENTS AND CONTRIBUTION

This book is built upon and provides a fresh update to existing sociological research on the book business and book culture, on the one hand, and on the broader processes of cultural production and consumption, on the other. Its contribution to scholarship is grounded in three key sets of findings and arguments:

1. The rise of independent bookstores in China should be understood as a cultural-economic process driven by two major forces: the bookstores' cultural objective of reasserting culture's central and autonomous role in the Chinese book retailing and broader cultural production fields, and their economic objective of differentiating themselves from competitors in order to cultivate a competitive advantage enabling them to survive in the highly competitive bookselling industry.

2. In pursuing these objectives, independent bookstores employ three *culturally adapted strategies*: political framing, moral positioning, and cultural distinguishing. These strategies enable them to fulfill both their cultural and economic goals by establishing a differentiating identity from competitors and creating a unique appeal to customers.

3. Similar to other "fields" in the Bourdieusian sense, the field of independent bookselling is shaped by power struggles between actors occupying different positions, holding varying types and quantities of resources, and driven by differing motives. This heterogeneity gives rise to varied attitudes toward commercialism among independent booksellers. The field is thus divided between independent bookstores that embrace commercialist goals and practices as a strategy for survival and a means to mitigate political influence, and those that regard commercialism as an equally heteronomous force as political power and unwaveringly reject it. This nuanced dynamic is the key to understanding the development and practices of independent bookstores and also serves as a key driving force behind the evolution of this field.

This book makes several contributions to scholarship. First, the original concept of culturally adapted strategy offers a novel framework for critically analyzing the logic of a cultural business, such as publishing and bookselling. Drawing on Bourdieu's seminal work on cultural production, this concept extends it by bridging the schism between cultural and economic production central to Bourdieu's account, where the field of cultural production is understood as "the economic world reversed."[9] My concept instead highlights how cultural and economic logics are often coalesced in cultural businesses as opposed to operating as mutually canceling forces. Additionally, the three specific culturally adapted strategies that I identify—political framing, moral positioning, and cultural distinguishing—provide versatile analytical tools for investigating cultural businesses akin to independent bookselling, both within China and in comparable contexts globally.

Second, my analysis of the political framing strategy employed by independent bookstores contributes to the development of a more rigorous understanding of the cultural politics of nonstate-owned media and cultural production in China. As noted earlier, much of the existing English-language literature on this topic is shaped by a narrow resistance discourse, which portrays nonstate media and cultural creators as politically motivated and ideologically driven to challenge the state and state-sanctioned practice and order in the Chinese media and cultural fields. In contrast to this simplified view, my analysis shows that much of the so-called political contestation exhibited by nonstate media and cultural participants, such as independent bookstores, should be more precisely understood as an act of political framing—a strategic tool used to advance their cultural and economic objectives rather than to fulfill confrontational political agendas. My perspective thus offers a more objective and critical-realist approach to understanding the cultural politics of nonstate media and cultural production in China.[10]

Finally, this book makes a significant contribution to the English-language literature on the sociological study of the book business and book culture. Until now, the most influential works in this field have been Miller's *Reluctant Capitalists* (2006) and Thompson's *Merchants of Culture* (2010). However, both monographs focus on the book industry in the English-speaking world, primarily the United States and the United Kingdom. This book is the first comprehensive sociological analysis of developments in the Chinese book industry, and it situates and critically analyzes the rise of independent bookstores within the broader social, cultural, economic, political, and historical transformations that have shaped China over the past four decades. This book will be of interest to scholars in cultural sociology, economic sociology, publishing studies, and China studies, as well as book industry practitioners seeking a deeper understanding of how societal dynamics shape the Chinese book industry, market, and culture.

WHAT FOLLOWS

Chapter 1 provides an overview of the basic structure of China's book industry, covering key areas including publishing, distribution, wholesaling, and retailing. Serving as a foundational introduction, this chapter offers essential background knowledge for readers unfamiliar with the organization and operations of the Chinese book industry to understand the findings and analyses discussed in the later chapters.

Chapter 2 offers a thorough examination of the concept of "independent bookstore" as it is understood and applied in the Chinese context. It focuses on how independent booksellers define, interpret, and enact their independent identity, as well as the debates surrounding it. The chapter shows that the term "independent bookstore"—*duli shudian* in Chinese—carries a richer and more nuanced meaning in the Chinese book industry compared to its more straightforward interpretation in the UK and US book trades. This richer connotation reflects the complex relationships that shape the evolution of independent bookselling in China and offers a valuable lens for examining these relationships and their historical roots.

Chapter 3 introduces the concept of "culturally adapted strategy" as a central analytical framework for understanding the practices of independent bookstores in China. In particular, I identify and examine three specific culturally adapted strategies: political framing, moral positioning, and cultural distinguishing. I argue that these strategies underlie and shape all major business activities of independent bookstores and are crucial for understanding these organizations. In addition to analyzing the strategies, I explore their deeper cultural, historical, political, and economic origins, showing how the rise of independent bookstores is deeply embedded in and shaped by

China's rich cultural traditions and evolving social, political, and economic trends and landscapes.

Chapter 4 provides a detailed account of how independent bookstores implement these culturally adapted strategies in their daily operations. In particular, it examines how these strategies affect the way that independent bookstores select books, organize events, and design and decorate their stores—the three key areas in which independent bookstores use these strategies to cultivate a unique appeal that serves to both distinguish them from their competitors and better attract customers.

In chapter 5, I turn to the economic dimensions of independent bookstores, focusing on how they generate revenue and maintain financial sustainability. The chapter begins by addressing the significant challenge faced by most independent bookstores: the difficulty of stocking books and turning a profit through book sales. I term the challenge "the conundrum of bookselling." This conundrum is the key to understanding the economic strategies of independent bookstores, especially why and how they decide to diversify into nonbook business lines, collaborate with shopping malls to secure rent reductions, and derive subsidies from various sources.

Together, these chapters provide a systematic analysis of independent bookstores as a unique and evolving phenomenon in the Chinese book industry. It highlights how independent bookstores both shape and are shaped by the evolution of the unique book culture and dynamic cultural production and consumption processes in China in the twenty-first century.

1

BOOK PUBLISHING AND RETAILING IN CHINA

This chapter provides a comprehensive overview of the basic structures of the book publishing and retailing industries in China.[1] These structures, alongside the practices embedded in them, have played an important role in shaping the rise of independent bookselling. Understanding them is, therefore, crucial for understanding the development and practices of independent bookstores. Furthermore, this chapter can be read as a concise yet comprehensive standalone account of the organization and operations of the Chinese book industry—an account currently lacking in the English-language literature.

BOOK PUBLISHING

The book publishing industry in China is characterized by a unique configuration where two distinct types of publishers coexist and closely collaborate with one another despite exhibiting marked differences between them. These are state-owned publishing houses, on the one hand, and privately owned book publishing companies, on the other hand. First, the state-owned publishing houses are the only entities in China with a legal status as "publishing house," or *chubanshe* in Chinese. In contrast, privately owned book publishing companies are usually referred to as "book companies," or *tushu gongsi*, suggesting their different legal status from the state-owned publishing house. Qualifying as a publishing house is important because it determines whether an organization has the legal right to publish books.

In order to publish books in China, publishers must apply to the National Press and Publication Administration (NPPA) for designated China Standard Book Numbers (henceforth CSBNs or book numbers) for the specific books they wish to publish.[2] Publishing books without valid book numbers is an offense. However, according to *Regulations on Publication Administration (Chuban Guangli Tiaoli)*, only a *chubanshe* is eligible to apply for book numbers. This effectively means that privately owned book publishing companies cannot apply for book numbers and, therefore, have no legal right to publish books. Nevertheless, in practice, there are mechanisms allowing privately owned book companies to circumvent this requirement and publish books without violating the law. The most common practice is for a privately owned book publishing company to pay a state house to use their book numbers to publish their own books—a practice commonly known as "book number sale," or *shuhao maimai*. It is through mechanisms like this that state-owned and privately owned publishers coexist and work closely together to shape the unique landscape of the Chinese book publishing industry.

State-Owned Publishing Houses

In 2021, there were a total of 587 state-owned publishing houses in China. This number has remained relatively stable over time, having increased only slightly from 573 in 2006 (see table 1.1).

TABLE 1.1 NUMBERS OF STATE-OWNED PUBLISHING HOUSES, 2006-2021

Year	Number of state-owned publishing houses	Year	Number of state-owned publishing houses
2006	573	2014	583
2007	578	2015	584
2008	579	2016	584
2009	580	2017	585
2010	581	2018	585
2011	580	2019	585
2012	580	2020	586
2013	582	2021	587

Source: NPPA

This stability can be attributed to two factors. First, as state-owned enterprises (SOEs), these publishing houses enjoy great financial security and stability, making closures due to financial difficulties extremely rare. The few cases of publishing houses that did close were due to noneconomic factors, primarily for consistently publishing books considered low-quality. This led to their deregistration by the NPPA for failing to fulfill the social duty of producing high-quality cultural goods.

Second, the threshold for establishing a publishing house in China is exceedingly high, requiring approval from the NPPA and its provincial branches, the Bureau of Press and Publication. According to the *Regulations on Publication Administration*, to set up a new publishing house, the applicant must first submit their proposal to the corresponding provincial-level Bureau of Press and Publication for initial review. If the bureau supports the application, it then forwards it to the NPPA for final approval. The ultimate authority to grant approval rests with the NPPA, not the provincial bureau. A crucial assessment criterion is whether the applicant has secured an eligible supervising organ (*zhuguan jiguan*) to oversee the operations of the proposed publishing house once it is established. Applications without such an arrangement are automatically rejected. Importantly, only state-affiliated entities—such as government departments, major state-funded universities, and state-owned enterprises—qualify as eligible supervising organs. As a result, it is practically impossible for privately owned companies or individuals to establish new publishing houses. This requirement is the second reason for the lack of fluctuation in the number of publishing houses in China over the years.

Of the total 587 publishing houses in 2021, 220 were classified as central-level publishing houses, and 367 were regional-level publishing houses. The distinction between these two categories does not necessarily stem from factors such as company size (many central-level publishing houses are small specialist publishers), market share (some regional-level houses rank among the largest publishers in China), market coverage (regional-level publishers can operate nationally), or any other economic attributes. Instead, the key differentiator consists in the nature of their supervising organ. Specifically, central-level publishing houses are those whose supervising organs are central-level entities, such as central government ministries, major organs of the Chinese Communist Party (CCP), the eight nonruling democratic parties, leading universities, or large centrally owned SOEs. Most of these central-level publishing houses are headquartered in Beijing. Examples include World Affairs Press, supervised by the Ministry of Foreign Affairs; the Central Compilation and Translation Press, which operates under the CCP's Central Compilation and Translation Bureau; Tsinghua University

Press; and CITIC Press Group, a subsidiary of CITIC Group, a major centrally owned SOE.

In contrast, regional-level publishing houses are supervised by regional supervising organs and are typically located in the capital cities of the thirty-two provincial administrative units in the Chinese mainland (twenty-three provinces, four autonomous regions, and five municipalities). Prior to the corporatization reform, which took place in most regional-level publishing houses during the 2000s and 2010s, the vast majority of regional-level publishing houses were owned and financed by their respective provincial or municipal governments and operated as public service organizations (*shiye danwei*) rather than for-profit enterprises. Today, most regional-level publishing houses operate as for-profit companies and are owned and managed by their respective provincial publishing groups. A provincial publishing group acts as the parent company for all publishing houses operating within the same provincial unit. Similarly, most central-level publishing houses have also undergone corporatization reforms and now operate as for-profit enterprises, although there remains a small number of central-level publishing houses that continue to run as public service organizations, fully funded by their supervising organs.

The corporatization reforms in the book publishing industry began in the early 2000s. Its primary goal was to transform publicly funded publishing houses into self-sufficient modern enterprises to enhance productivity in the sector.[3] A secondary goal was to facilitate the creation of large regional publishing groups through the amalgamation of individual publishing houses operating within the same provincial units. The first such publishing group was Shanghai Century Publishing Group, established in 1999 by the Shanghai Municipal Government through the consolidation of the five publishing houses it owned into a single publishing conglomerate. Following this model, most of the thirty-two provinces, autonomous regions, and municipalities implemented similar reforms, creating their own provincial publishing groups. Some of these groups have since grown into major global players in the publishing industry. Prominent examples include Jiangsu Phoenix Publishing & Media Group and China South Publishing & Media Group, both of which consistently rank among the largest publishing corporations in the world. At the central level, China Publishing Group (CPG) was established in Beijing in 2002. It is now the largest publishing group in China, with over ninety subsidiaries, including fourteen central-level publishing houses.

A Chinese publishing house tends to have a similar organizational structure as a typical publishing house in the United Kingdom or the United States, consisting of key departments such as editorial, design, production, marketing, and sales. The publishing process is also similar, including commissioning, manuscript editing, design, production, distribution, marketing, sales, and so on. The editorial department plays a pivotal role in acquiring and evaluating manuscripts, working closely with authors to create and prepare content for publication. The design and production departments focus on creating visually appealing layouts and cover designs while maintaining high-quality printing standards, and the marketing and sales departments are responsible for promoting and selling books to maximize sales and profits. Overall, although there may be cultural and contextual nuances unique to Chinese publishing houses, their core publishing processes and practices largely align with those of Western publishers, underlain by the same objective of producing and disseminating books to readers effectively.

A notable distinction between book publishing in China and the English-speaking world lies in the way the industry is categorized. In English-speaking countries, publishing is typically divided into two broad sectors: trade or general interest publishing, on the one hand, and nonconsumer publishing, which includes educational, academic, STM (scientific, technical, and medical), and professional publishing, on the other.[4] In contrast, Chinese book publishing classifies books into eight (sometimes nine) categories: social sciences, science and technology, literature and art, children's books, Chinese classics, education, academic, and references and encyclopedias.[5] Each category may include both trade books and publications aimed at specialist audiences. For instance, within the social sciences category, one might find both academic monographs on social science topics (these books may also be found under the academic category) and general interest books concerning social life generally, such as self-help guides. In recent years, Western categories like fiction and nonfiction have been adopted by some Chinese publishers as a simpler way of distinguishing between different types of books, although distinctions like those between paperback and hardcover publishing remain largely irrelevant in the Chinese book publishing field.

In the past, a Chinese publishing house only published books in its assigned subject area. This was often reflected in the publisher's name. For example, Shanghai Literature and Art Publishing House would primarily publish in the field of literature and art, whereas Metallurgical Industry Press was established to publish books relevant to the steel industry. Today, more and more publishing houses are publishing outside of their original subject areas. For instance, China Machine Press, originally established to publish science and technology monographs, has evolved into a leading publisher of translated economics and management textbooks and monographs. This cross-over was partially driven by the corporatization reforms, which required publishing houses to become more financially self-sufficient through market competition. Many publishing houses thus have chosen to diversify into fields with higher market demand to remain competitive. Another factor has to do with the role of state houses as proxies for privately owned book publishing companies. Many of the books published by state-owned houses are, in fact, produced by privately owned book companies, which use state houses' book numbers and other resources to publish the content they create.

Privately Owned Book Publishing Companies

As noted earlier, privately owned book companies in China cannot legally publish books independently because, without the legal status of a "publishing house," they cannot apply for book numbers. However, private companies are permitted to engage in most other core publishing activities, including planning, commissioning, contracting, editing, production, distributing, and marketing. Therefore, for a privately owned book company to publish books legally, all it has to do is "collaborate" with a state-owned publishing house and publish its books using the state house's book numbers. This practice is commonly referred to as "collaborative publishing," or *hezuo chuban*.

In practice, collaborative publishing can take several forms. During the 1990s and 2000s, the most prevalent form involved the direct transfer of book numbers from state-owned publishing houses to privately owned book companies, called "book number sale" (*shuhao maimai*). Under this arrangement, the state house would set a price for its book numbers, which private companies could pay to acquire. In the 2000s, the cost of a book number typically ranged from 10,000 to 30,000 yuan (approximately

US$1,394–4,182),[6] with factors like the state house's reputation (more reputable houses commanded higher prices) influencing the price. In the past decade, due to the controversial legality of this practice, direct book number sales have become somewhat secretive, with the specific pricing details often kept confidential to outsiders. However, according to accounts I gathered from book editors and booksellers, the average price of a book number in the 2010s generally ranged from 15,000 to 50,000 yuan (approximately US$2,091–6,970).

The declining popularity of direct book number sales in recent years is due to a major change in how book numbers are allocated to publishing houses. Before 2009, all state-owned publishing houses received a fixed bundle of book numbers at the beginning of each year, typically ranging from 500 to 2000. This system allowed publishing houses to have access to book numbers even before they had specific books ready for publication. The allocation of book numbers to each publishing house was determined by several factors, such as the house's operational level (central-level publishing houses were typically given more book numbers than regional-level houses), the size of the house, and the sector or subject area it specialized in. For instance, publishers of educational books generally received more book numbers due to the larger size of the educational book market. As a result, there were considerable variations in the quantities of book numbers allocated to different publishing houses. Meanwhile, publishing houses were not allowed to carry forward unused book numbers to the following year. A large surplus of unused book numbers could result in a reduction in the next year's allocation, for the NPPA interpreted this surplus as evidence that the allocation exceeded the house's publishing capacity. On the other hand, publishing houses that exhausted all their allocated book numbers before the year-end had the ability to apply for additional numbers, which would then lead to a larger allocation in the following year. These mechanisms inadvertently incentivized publishing houses to engage in book number sales, in that the more book numbers they consumed in a year—whether by using them to publish books or by selling them to private companies—the more numbers they could receive in the following year. According to several book trade insiders I spoke to, in the 1990s and 2000s, many small regional-level publishing houses sold more book numbers than they actually used for publishing books.

A new book number allocation method was introduced in 2009 to address these issues. Today, publishing houses no longer receive a guaranteed annual bundle of book numbers. Instead, they must apply for book numbers on a one-book-one-number (*yishu yihao*) basis. Under the new system, publishing houses can only apply for a book number once the manuscript has successfully passed the three-step examination (*sanshenzhi*) and is ready for production.[7] This shift has increased the state house's involvement in the private book company's projects, for in order to apply for a book number, a state-house editor must use a dedicated online application system to submit detailed information about the book concerned, including its title, author, price, synopsis, target market, proposed publication date, and more. Moreover, the acceptance or rejection of these applications can have an impact on the publishing house's future applications, incentivizing greater quality control. As a result, many state houses now demand higher levels of oversight and involvement in private companies' projects from the early stages to minimize the risk of rejected applications.

All these changes have rendered direct book number sales increasingly unpopular and impractical, and alternative models of collaborative publishing are on the rise. One popular model involves the privately owned book company providing the state house with complimentary copies of the books they publish together instead of making direct monetary remuneration. This arrangement not only works better under the new book number application system but also helps to mitigate the legal risks associated with direct book number sales. Here is how it works: Let's say state house A and private company B agree to collaborate to publish a book with a list price of 40 yuan. The project costs a total of 20,000 yuan. Instead of direct payment, B agrees to give A three thousand free copies of the book. A then sells these copies to its distributors and wholesalers at a 50 percent discount, generating a revenue of 60,000 yuan. After deducting the project cost of 20,000 yuan, A is left with a net profit of 40,000 yuan from this collaboration. This profit serves effectively as the fee paid by B to A for using A's book number and other publishing resources to publish the book.

Large privately owned book companies with their own production, distribution, marketing, and sales facilities are more inclined to adopt this model as it allows them to retain a greater share of the profits. In certain cases, instead of receiving free copies, the state-owned publishing house may have to purchase copies from the private company, though at a significantly reduced price—often as low as 25 percent of the list price—and then sell these copies at market rates to generate profit. This arrangement typically occurs when the private company, rather than the state house, holds a stronger negotiating position in the partnership. Conversely, when the private company is smaller and relies heavily on the state house's production, distribution, marketing, and other facilities—hence incurring higher costs for the state house—they may divide the copies in such a way that the state house secures a larger share of the profits from the project. In such cases, the private company generates its profits by selling its allocated copies to small, privately owned book wholesalers and retailers, while the state house makes a large profit by selling its copies to large regional or national distributors and wholesalers and Xinhua Bookstores—these are the exclusive clients of state-owned publishing houses, which privately owned companies are not permitted to supply.

In addition to adopting new collaboration models, it has become increasingly common for state-owned publishing houses or the publishing groups owning them to hold shares in or acquire competitive private companies. A notable example is the 2015 acquisition of CS-Booky by China South Publishing & Media Group, which led to the formation of China South CS-Booky Cultural Media Co Ltd. Before this acquisition, CS-Booky, a highly regarded privately owned book publishing company, was widely recognized as a top publisher in the social sciences. One result of such mergers and acquisitions in the publishing field is the blurring of boundaries between state-owned publishing houses and privately owned book companies. These entities, which once operated as distinct players in the Chinese publishing field, increasingly function as interconnected units. The ability to apply for book numbers remains perhaps the only clear distinction between state-owned and privately owned publishers. However, even this difference becomes less relevant when state-owned houses acquire private companies and operate them as their imprints. Through such acquisitions, state-owned publishing houses gain access to valuable resources held by private companies, such as established author networks and specialized expertise, while private companies benefit from easier access to book numbers and the regulatory advantages of operating under a state-owned entity. This synergy enhances the competitiveness and market reach of both parties.

BOOK DISTRIBUTION AND WHOLESALING

Before delving into the structure of the book retailing industry in China, it is essential to first consider the processes through which books move from publishers to retailers. Book distributors and wholesalers play a critical role in linking publishers with retailers and ensuring that new books reach the retail market efficiently and in a timely manner. Nevertheless, their roles and practices are often overlooked in scholarly discussions of the Chinese book business.

If you are a brick-and-mortar general interest bookseller in China, there are several ways to procure stock for your bookshop. If your shop is small and newly established, your stocking options will be somewhat limited. Instead of ordering copies directly from your preferred publishers, you are more likely to begin by sourcing books from those large online book retailing platforms. You may also find yourself regularly visiting or calling your local book wholesalers to stay informed about new stock arrivals. Over time, your wholesalers may offer you a credit account, which allows you to defer payment within a specified credit period rather than making immediate cash payments. This arrangement is attractive to bookstores with limited cash flow but is not always available to all bookstores, especially the small and newly established ones. On the other hand, if you are fortunate enough to have successfully run your bookstore for several years and have expanded it into a medium-sized or large establishment, you now have the option to order books directly from publishers or from the large regional or national book distributors they work with. Both scenarios, however, assume that you work for a privately owned bookstore. If, instead, you work at a state-owned Xinhua Bookstore, your experience in stocking would be very different. In particular, as a Xinhua Bookstore employee, your main role would involve accepting and selling stock that has been centrally ordered for you by your provincial or municipal Xinhua Bookstore head stores rather than independently sourcing books for your store.

As with the publishing sector, the book distribution and wholesaling industry in China is also characterized by a demarcation between state-owned and privately owned players. Publishers commonly refer to state-owned distributors and wholesalers as the main channel (*zhu qudao*) and private distributors and wholesalers as the secondary channel (*er qudao*) to distinguish them.

The main channel comprises the state-owned Xinhua Bookstore system, publishing houses' self-run retail outlets, and the China Post system (which primarily serves the postal book market). Among these, the Xinhua Bookstore system is the most important player. As I will show shortly, Xinhua Bookstore is the leading book retailer in China. Currently, there are over ten thousand Xinhua Bookstore retail stores nationwide, which are owned and operated by their respective provincial Xinhua Bookstore Groups. Within these provincial Xinhua Bookstore Groups, the typical organizational structure tends to include a provincial head store (*shengdian*), a municipal head store (*shidian*), and numerous retail stores operating in the province concerned. The two head stores function as distributors, sourcing books from publishers and distributing them to the retail stores they manage. The difference between the provincial and municipal head stores lies in their jurisdiction. The municipal head store, typically located in the provincial capital (hence its name), oversees and supplies the retail stores in the capital city. In contrast, the provincial head store manages and supplies all other Xinhua Bookstore retail stores in the rest of the province.

From publishers' perspective, especially state-owned publishing houses, the two Xinhua Bookstore head stores in each province constitute their most important clients. They rely on the approximately sixty Xinhua Bookstore head stores across the country to distribute their books (see figure 1.1). Commenting on this, a sales manager from a medium-sized regional publishing house whom I interviewed remarked: "My main job is sending books to the sixty or so Xinhua Bookstore head stores, day in, day out."

Some publishing houses distribute books solely through the Xinhua Bookstore system, while others also supply books to privately owned distributors, wholesalers, and retailers. These private players constitute the secondary channel. The term *secondary* implies that, compared to the main channel, the private market is considered less important by state-owned publishers. This perception was especially prevalent in the 1990s and early 2000s before the emergence of online bookstores. Back then, state-owned publishers often regarded privately owned channels

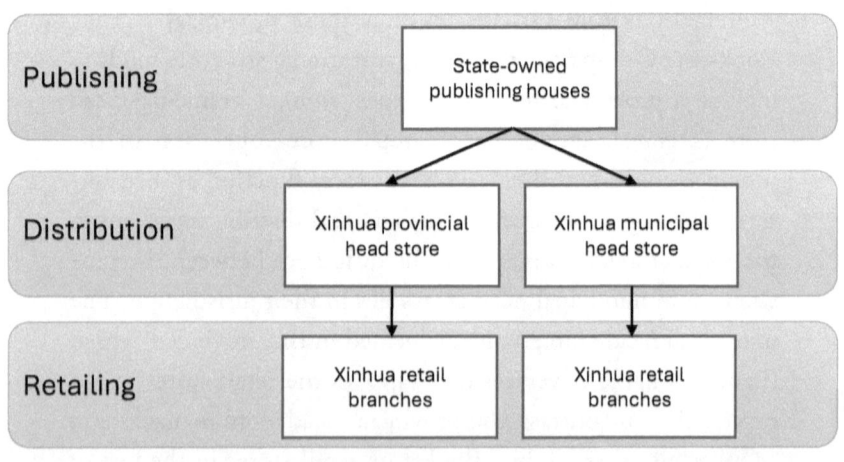

FIGURE 1.1 The main channel

as playing a merely supplementary role to Xinhua Bookstore. As a result, many were reluctant to engage with private players due to their small market share. This disconnection between state-owned publishers and small privately owned book wholesalers and retailers was noticed by some larger privately owned wholesalers. Recognizing this gap, some companies pivoted to focus on the private market and have gone on to develop into large regional or national book distributors, specializing in sourcing books from state-owned publishers and supplying them to smaller, privately owned wholesalers and retailers. They are known as "middle dealer" (*zhongpanshang*), a term highlighting their intermediary role in the book distribution and wholesaling landscape (see figure 1.2).

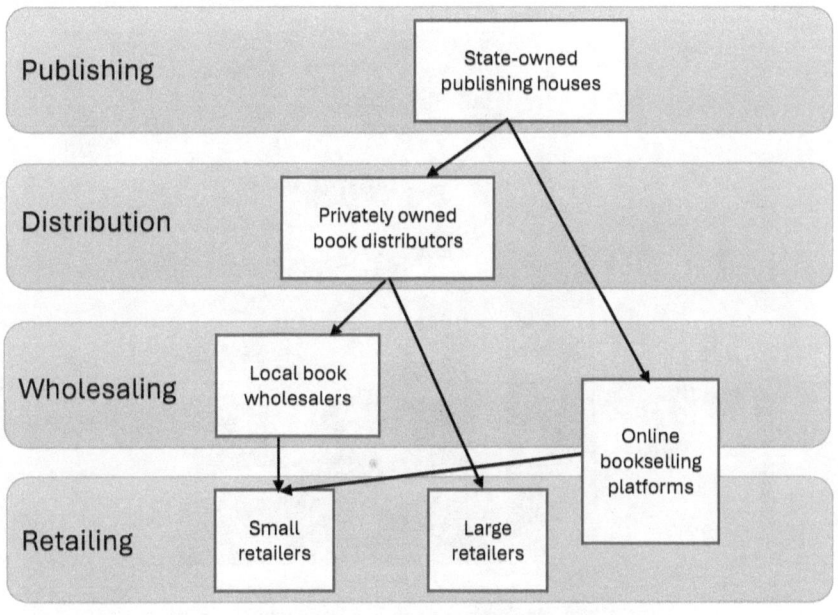

FIGURE 1.2 The secondary channel

Private distributors mainly serve local book wholesalers and large bookstores. Local book wholesalers cater to small- and medium-sized bookstores. Local book wholesalers are often located in facilities known as book wholesale centers (*tushu pifa shichang*), which are common in large cities across China, such as the provincial capitals and other major cities in a province. A book wholesale center functions similarly to a large shopping mall, housing up to hundreds of individual shops operated by book wholesalers who trade with both bookstores and individual consumers (see figure 1.3). These shops typically serve multiple purposes: as retail spaces, offices, and stock rooms, with additional warehouse space often available to the wholesalers located in the same center. Most book wholesalers trading in these

FIGURE 1.3 A wholesaler's shop in a book wholesale center

Source: SZ Days

wholesale centers are considered small- to medium-sized businesses and usually specialize in specific types of books, such as children's books or educational books.

Large privately owned bookstores can stock books directly from publishers and distributors, benefitting from higher discounts and faster delivery services. However, the vast majority of privately owned bookstores are small- to medium-sized and rely heavily on their local book wholesalers for a steady supply of stock. Two variations merit attention. First, the emergence of large online bookselling platforms has provided small- to medium-sized privately owned bookstores with an alternative avenue for acquiring stock. These platforms typically stock books directly from publishers at highly competitive rates, enabling them to resell books to small book retailers at discounted prices while still maintaining profitability. Additionally, these platforms frequently host special sales events, offering books at exceptionally low prices and making them an economical choice for inventory stocking for small bookstores. Nearly all the independent bookstores I studied reported having purchased inventory from these websites. Second, in the case of books published collaboratively by privately owned book publishing companies and state-owned publishing houses, distribution practices differ. Typically, the private company sells its share of copies through the secondary channel, while the state house handles its share of copies via the main channel (as previously noted, in a "collaborative publishing" project, copies are often divided between the state house and the private company). With the increasing prevalence of warehouse automation and reduced logistics costs, an increasing number of privately owned book publishing companies are now willing to directly supply books to small- and medium-sized bookstores, including independent bookstores.

Let's conclude this section by briefly discussing the terms of trade in book distribution and wholesale. In terms of discounts, as a rule of thumb, state-owned publishing houses typically offer discounts ranging between 50–55 percent off the list price to Xinhua Bookstore provincial head stores and large regional or national distributors. Xinhua Bookstore municipal head stores and large online bookselling websites receive slightly lower discounts, between 40–45 percent. Local book wholesalers and large privately owned bookstores, when dealing directly with publishers, are typically offered discounts of 30–35 percent. For small- to medium-sized privately owned bookstores sourcing stock from local book wholesalers or directly from publishers on a cash payment basis, the usual discount falls within the range of 28–35 percent. Discount rates can vary significantly depending on the category or genre of books. Educational books and popular genres such as teen fiction often have much steeper discounts. The discount figures mentioned here apply to high-quality general interest and academic books, which are the types of books most commonly stocked by independent bookstores.

Regarding payment arrangements, Xinhua Bookstore head stores and distributors typically purchase books from publishers on consignment, meaning that they pay publishers periodically for the copies sold during the previous credit period and have the option to return unsold copies to the publishers. Xinhua Bookstore head stores enjoy the longest credit period of twelve months, or longer for certain types of books. This means that payments are typically settled annually for books sold over the past year. Distributors usually receive shorter credit periods of three to six months. Large online bookselling websites are typically granted a credit period of three months but do not have the right to return unsold copies. Instead, they may exchange unsold stock for new books of equivalent value. In contrast, small, privately owned book wholesalers and retailers that purchase books directly from publishers are often required to pay in cash without the option of returns or exchanges. These terms of trade highlight the stratified dynamics of the book industry, where conditions are shaped by the scale and market power of the participants involved.

BOOK RETAILING

Ordinary readers in China have a variety of options when it comes to purchasing books. The state-owned Xinhua Bookstores are typically the largest and best-stocked physical bookstores in most Chinese cities and towns. These stores usually carry an extensive inventory, including both frontlist and backlist titles. The books in Xinhua Bookstores are generally sold at full price without discounts. Privately owned bookstores, however, come in varied sizes, ranging from small specialist bookshops to regional chains. These stores usually offer modest discounts of 5–10 percent. Readers looking for steeper discounts can go to their local book wholesale centers, where wholesalers are often willing to sell books at a 20 percent discount, even for single-copy purchases. Customers looking for even greater savings frequently turn to the internet, where large online bookselling websites are known for selling books at heavily discounted prices. In addition to these channels, some supermarkets also sell books. However, the supermarket book market in China is quite small and not comparable to that in countries like the United States and the United Kingdom, where large chain supermarkets can sell hundreds of thousands of copies.[8]

In this section, I examine the three major types of retail bookstores in China today: the state-owned Xinhua Bookstore, privately owned bookstores, and large online bookselling websites.

The State-Owned Xinhua Bookstore

The first Xinhua Bookstore was established in 1937 in Yan'an, Shaanxi Province, as the official publication distribution organ of the Chinese Communist Party (CCP). Today, the brand name Xinhua Bookstore is shared by over ten thousand retail Xinhua bookstores. These bookstores are owned and managed by their respective provincial Xinhua Bookstore Groups. Although these bookstores share the same brand name, each Xinhua Bookstore Group functions as an independent business entity. For example, Shandong Xinhua Bookstore Group and Henan Xinhua Bookstore Group are distinct companies operating independently. Most Xinhua Bookstore Groups limit their operations to their respective provinces, although some larger Groups, such as Sichuan Xinhua Winshare Publishing and Media Group in Sichuan Province, provide nationwide services. However, these services are primarily provided via their online bookselling offerings rather than by operating physical bookstores in other provinces. Many Xinhua Bookstore Groups are themselves part of their provincial publishing groups. For example, Sichuan Xinhua Winshare Publishing and Media Group is a subsidiary of Sichuan Xinhua Publishing Group.

Xinhua Bookstore as a whole is the largest book retailer in China. In 2019, the combined sales of the Xinhua Bookstore system and publishing houses' self-run retail outlets totaled 8.5 billion copies of books worth 109.066 billion yuan.[9] Given the minuscule market share of the latter—only 392 publisher-run retail outlets existed nationwide in 2019—it is reasonable to conclude that the majority of these sales were generated by Xinhua Bookstores. A key characteristic of Xinhua Bookstore is its heavy reliance on the sale of educational books, primarily school textbooks and study aid books (*jiaofushu*, or exam prep guides). As illustrated in figures 1.4 and 1.5, the educational book market is the largest submarket in the Chinese book publishing and retailing industries, and Xinhua Bookstore occupies a dominant position in this highly profitable market segment. In particular, Xinhua enjoys a near monopoly in the school textbook market, having been the exclusive distributor and retailer of these books for decades. Although not the sole player in the study aid book market, Xinhua Bookstore sells a large volume of these books and makes substantial profits from these sales.

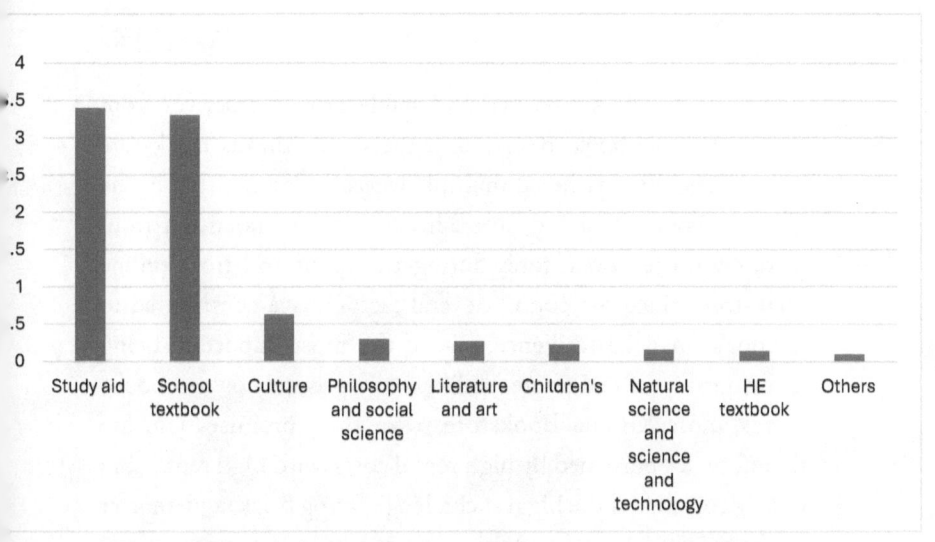

FIGURE 1.4 Xinhua Bookstore book sales by copy in 2019 (unit: billion)

Source: NPPA (2020)

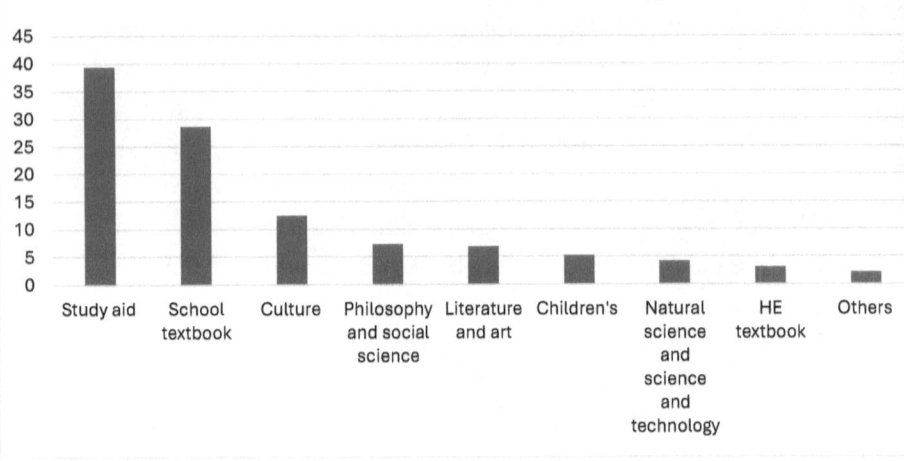

FIGURE 1.5 Xinhua Bookstore book sales by value in 2019 (unit: billion, yuan)

Source: NPPA (2020)

Thanks to the substantial and stable profits it derives from the educational book market, over the years, Xinhua Bookstore has successfully weathered multiple waves of competition in the Chinese bookselling industry. This includes competition from privately owned bookstores during the 1990s and from online bookstores since the 2000s. Several factors have contributed to Xinhua's financial resilience, one of the most important being its ownership of real estate. Unlike many privately owned bookstores, most Xinhua Bookstores own their premises and are therefore not burdened by high rental costs, with high rent being widely considered the biggest challenge facing brick-and-mortar bookstores in China. In addition to not having to pay rent, many Xinhua Bookstores generate extra revenue by leasing out portions of their real estate. Furthermore, Xinhua Bookstores operating in prefectural-level towns and rural areas have always benefitted from exemptions from value-added tax (VAT), a policy advantage that privately owned physical bookstores did not enjoy until 2013. The combination of these factors has greatly bolstered Xinhua's financial strength, enabling it to maintain resilience in the face of competition and volatile market conditions.

However, Xinhua's advantageous market position and financial stability have also drawn criticism from customers and industry observers, who perceive a lack of innovation and commitment to delivering excellent customer service in the industry leader. Common complaints include the outdated interior design of many Xinhua Bookstores and the overly large inventories that make it difficult for readers to locate specific titles. Critics argue that the chain has been complacent in enhancing the shopping experience and unwisely prioritizes functionality over customer appeal. Figure 1.6 shows a typical Xinhua Bookstore that would

FIGURE 1.6 A typical Xinhua Bookstore
Source: Shandong Xinhua Bookstore Group

be subject to these criticisms. While the store is perfectly functional, it lacks inviting features or facilities that would make shopping a more enjoyable experience for customers.

Many attribute these shortcomings to Xinhua Bookstore's intrinsic lack of customer care. However, when we think about this, it is important to consider the wider context behind Xinhua's prioritization of functionality over aesthetics. Historically, Xinhua Bookstores operated as public service organizations with the responsibility of displaying in their stores literally *all* books sent to them by publishers from all over the country for customers to browse and purchase. Although now operating as for-profit businesses, Xinhua Bookstores continue to serve as crucial display windows for publishers and books. They play a vital role in sustaining the visibility and availability of books that may not get stocked by market-driven retailers. This obligation limits Xinhua's ability to curate its stock as selectively as privately owned bookstores. Instead, Xinhua Bookstores must maximize their shelf space to accommodate the vast amount of titles they receive from publishers nationwide. This focus on functionality over aesthetics reflects and embeds the state bookseller's enduring role as a vital bridge between publishers and readers rather than as a purely customer- and market-driven enterprise.

That being said, in recent years, Xinhua Bookstores have increasingly begun to modernize their stores. This shift has been partly driven by the influence of independent bookstores, which, as I shall discuss later, have been pioneers in the Chinese bookselling field by creating visually appealing store environments and offering diverse in-store services. Recognizing the need to adapt to changing consumer expectations, many Xinhua Bookstores have drawn inspiration from independent bookstores, investing heavily in store renovations and expanding their offerings to include a wider variety of products and services (see figure 1.7).

FIGURE 1.7 A fully redecorated Xinhua Bookstore
Source: Shandong Xinhua Bookstore Group

Privately Owned Bookstores

Privately owned bookstores first emerged in China during the late 1970s and early 1980s, initially taking the form of small book vendors and book booths. These modest enterprises were typically run by unemployed school graduates who lacked stable jobs in state-owned factories or public service organizations—these jobs were considered more desirable than self-employment at the time. However, despite the perceived disadvantages of running a business, private bookselling quickly proved to be a financially rewarding venture. This is because, in the pre-internet era, when even television was a luxury for most Chinese households, books were a popular medium for both learning and entertainment. Demand for books was so high that readers would queue overnight outside bookstores in order to secure a copy of a newly released book, and, as Qingguo Sun, a veteran publisher, recalls, "Every book published would be welcomed by readers and sell out in no time."[10] This thriving market attracted more people to the bookselling business, leading to a significant expansion of privately run bookstores in China during the 1980s. By 1987, there were an estimated ten thousand privately owned book booths or bookstores across the country, approximately 1.18 times the number of state-owned Xinhua Bookstore branches.[11]

The privately owned bookselling market continued to grow throughout the 1990s, culminating at 35,282 bookstores nationwide in 1999, approximately four times the number of Xinhua Bookstores.[12] In addition to small- to medium-sized individually-run bookstores, this period also saw the emergence of large chain bookstores. Xishu Bookstore, for example, became an industry leader with over six hundred chain and franchise stores across the country by the late 1990s.

During the 1990s, privately owned bookstores grew not only in quantity but also in quality. One notable development was the rise of bookstores that specialized in high-quality academic and intellectual books in the humanities and social sciences. These books, collectively known as *xueshu shu*, or "scholarly books," encompassed both academic works written by and for academics and serious nonfiction books. Despite their specialist nature, these publications gained a wide readership during the 1980s and 1990s and shaped China's intellectual landscape over this period. The bookstores focusing on these books were referred to as *xueshu shudian*, or "scholarly bookstores," highlighting their dedication to providing high-quality academic and intellectually enriching books.[13] According to one interviewee who owned one such bookstore in the 1990s, approximately 1,500–1,600 scholarly bookstores were opened across China between 1993 and 1998.

The emergence of scholarly bookstores is noteworthy because they can be seen as precursors to today's independent bookstores. Their connection lies in a shared dedication to providing high-quality academic and intellectually nourishing publications. As I shall discuss in chapter 4, this commitment is a defining characteristic of independent bookstores. Recognizing the historical link between scholarly bookstores of the 1990s and contemporary independent bookstores allows us to contextualize our understanding of independent bookstores within a broader socio-historical framework and highlight their cultural roots and the enduring connections that shape their identity and purpose.

In summary, the 1990s marked a golden age for China's privately owned bookstores. During this period, commercially driven bookstores, which primarily sold popular and profitable titles such as study aid books, thrived alongside culturally oriented bookstores like scholarly bookstores. This decade witnessed a thriving and diverse book market that rewarded both commercial and cultural bookstores.

However, the prosperity of the 1990s began to wane with the advent of the new millennium. Many privately owned bookstores began to experience sharp declines in their book sales, leading to widespread bookstore closures. As shown in table 1.2, the number of privately owned bookstores fell by 8 percent, from 37,374 in 2000 to 34,483 in 2003. Although a change in 2004 in the methodology used by the NPPA to count the number of privately owned bookstores renders direct comparisons of data collected before and after this point untenable, the trend is clear: The 2000s was set to be a challenging decade for China's privately owned bookstores. Several interviewees described this period as their "winter," illustrating the scale of the challenges they experienced.

TABLE 1.2 NUMBERS OF PRIVATELY OWNED BOOKSTORES, 1994–2003

Year	Number	Change from previous year
1994	29,669	N/A
1995	33,415	+3,746
1996	35,534	+2,119
1997	35,827	+293
1998	35,450	–377
1999	35,282	–168
2000	37,374	+2,092
2001	36,448	–926 (2.4%)
2002	36,035	–413 (1.1%)
2003	34,384	–1,551 (4.3%)

Source: NPPA

Two factors contributed to this changing landscape. First, the rise of online bookstores in the early 2000s significantly disrupted the market. Offering lower prices and convenient delivery services, these powerful players created formidable competition for small brick-and-mortar bookstores, which struggled to match their pricing and accessibility. Second, the escalating real estate prices across China from the mid-2000s increased operational costs for bookstores who rented their premises, which compounded the financial strain caused by declining book sales. Together, these factors forced many privately owned bookstores to shut down, resulting in a significant reduction in their numbers and market share. According to a study conducted by Min Yu et al. in early the 2000s, privately owned bookstores accounted for 56.94 percent of China's book sales in 2002.[14] However, their market share sharply dropped to

23.5 percent, 33.3 percent, and 31 percent in 2014, 2015, and 2016, respectively, according to OpenBook's data.[15] These figures show the magnitude of the transformation experienced by privately owned bookstores throughout the 2000s and 2010s.

The contemporary private bookselling field in China is defined by a clear distinction between independent bookstores, on the one hand, and nonindependent privately owned bookstores, on the other hand. This distinction stems primarily from the different approaches these bookstores adopt to balance culture and commerce in book retailing. Independent bookstores position themselves as cultural creators and strive to prioritize and preserve cultural rules and values in bookselling by offering high-quality intellectual and literary publications and a diverse range of cultural activities and experiences. In contrast, nonindependent, privately owned bookstores typically prioritize sales and profits over cultural values. The differing philosophies and practices adopted by independent and nonindependent private bookstores hence shape not only the types of books and services available to customers but also the structure of the contemporary private bookselling field in China.

Online Book Retailing

The advent of online book retailing in China occurred at the turn of the new millennium, marked by the launches of Dangdang.com and Joyo.com in 1999 and 2000, respectively. Both websites were established as online bookstores focusing on selling books, magazines, and audio-visual products such as CDs. However, neither company made much impact until 2003. That year, the outbreak of the SARS (severe acute respiratory syndrome) virus hit China, leading to the implementation of lockdown measures, which inadvertently accelerated the growth of e-commerce in the country. With an increasing number of consumers choosing to shop online to avoid leaving their homes, Dangdang, Joyo, and other e-commerce platforms—such as Alibaba Group's Taobao.com and 1688.com—experienced significant growth.[16] Dangdang, for instance, reported a 30 percent increase in book sales in April 2003 compared to April 2002, while Joyo achieved more sales in the first week of May 2003 than it typically recorded in an entire month.[17] By the end of 2003, Dangdang's annual sales reached 100 million yuan (approximately US$13.94 million), marking a significant milestone in the development of China's online bookselling industry.

As the pioneering online bookstore in China, Dangdang shares similarities with Amazon.com. Just like Amazon, which operated at a loss for eight consecutive years following its launch in 1995,[18] Dangdang also experienced a decade of unprofitability. It was not until 2009 that it achieved its first profit of 10 million yuan (approximately US$1.57 million). However, after going public on the New York Stock Exchange (NYSE) in 2010, Dangdang immediately reverted to a state of financial loss, reporting deficits of 228 million yuan in 2011, 444 million yuan in 2012, and 143 million yuan in 2013.[19] The company managed to record a profit of 88 million yuan in 2014, but its struggles persisted. Unlike Amazon's eventual dominance in the US and global online bookselling landscape, Dangdang never achieved dominance in China's online bookselling field. Even at its peak, between the mid-2000s and the mid-2010s, Dangdang's market share never exceeded 50 percent. In 2016, it delisted from the NYSE, driven by internal conflicts between its founders and the ongoing struggle to compete effectively.

Dangdang's trajectory thus contrasts sharply with Amazon's triumphant rise. Despite being China's first online bookstore, it faced relentless competition from both other online bookstores (e.g., Joyo/Amazon China) and general e-commerce platforms, especially JD.com and Tmall. These challenges prevented Dangdang from ever attaining a dominant position in the Chinese online bookselling market.

In 2004, Amazon entered China by acquiring Joyo.com for $75 million. It subsequently transformed Joyo into its official Chinese website, rebranding it as Joyo Amazon and replacing the domain Joyo.com with Amazon.cn in 2007. The company adopted the brand name Amazon China in 2011. Initially, Amazon China was the second-largest online bookstore in the country. For example, in 2014, it commanded a 25 percent share of China's online book sales, ranking just behind Dangdang, which held a 41 percent share.[20] However, in the following years, Amazon China faced strong competition from JD.com and Tmall Books, which resulted in a rapid decline in its market position. In 2016, its market share dropped to 16 percent, while Dangdang retained a 45 percent share, and JD's share rose to 21 percent.[21] In April 2019, Amazon China closed down its domestic e-commerce operations, ceasing to sell goods sourced within China to Chinese consumers. This effectively marked Amazon China's withdrawal from the online bookselling market and an altogether exit from China's e-commerce.

Replacing Amazon China as the runner-ups were JD.com and Tmall.com. Both platforms had already established themselves as leading online retailers before venturing into online bookselling in the early 2010s, more than a decade after the launches of Dangdang and Joyo. However, despite their relatively late entry, both platforms swiftly rose to industry leaders.

JD.com was established in 2004 as an online retailer of 3C (computer, communication, and consumer electronics) products. It soon developed into one of China's leading online retailers, operating on a self-fulfillment model, meaning it buys and resells goods directly to customers. In contrast, Tmall.com is an e-commerce platform operated by Alibaba Group. It distinguishes itself from its sister site, Taobao.com, by hosting premium brands and larger companies, whereas Taobao mainly caters to small traders. By 2020, Tmall had become the largest e-commerce platform in China, hosting more than 220,000 stores, including globally recognized brands such as Huawei, Apple, Burberry, Audi, and many others. Unlike JD.com's self-fulfillment model, Tmall functions as a marketplace platform, enabling businesses to establish their own online stores to sell goods directly to consumers within the Tmall-Alibaba ecosystem.[22]

Tmall Books was launched in 2012 as Tmall's dedicated book department. Like the main site, Tmall Books operates as a platform for online bookstores rather than buying and selling books directly to consumers. By 2021, it had been home to over 3,900 bookstores. Strictly speaking, Tmall Books is not directly comparable to JD and Dangdang in that it does not fulfill book orders itself but instead facilitates transactions between bookstores and consumers. Nevertheless, to gauge its scale, Tmall Books facilitated book sales worth over 38.5 billion yuan (approximately US$6.03 billion) in 2020, making it the largest online bookselling platform in China.[23] In comparison, the entire brick-and-mortar bookselling sector generated 20.4 billion yuan in book sales that year. Such is Tmall Book's influence that even Dangdang opened a Tmall store in 2012.

To sum up, before the COVID-19 pandemic, the Chinese online bookselling market was largely dominated by Dangdang, JD.com, and Tmall Books. While Dangdang revolutionized China's book retailing industry by introducing online bookselling, JD.com and Tmall Books each brought other notable changes to the field.

The most important change brought about by JD.com was the normalization of heavy discounting. Before JD's entry into the market, both Dangdang and Amazon China offered discounts, but these were modest—typically ranging between 15 percent and 25 percent off the list price—allowing them to maintain comfortable gross profit margins of approximately 20 percent. However, JD.com disrupted this equilibrium. To compete with Dangdang's market leadership, JD not only matched Dangdang's prices but also introduced aggressive promotions, such as 50 yuan off when spending 100 yuan and 100 yuan off when spending 200 yuan, to further bring prices down. On December 14, 2010, shortly after Dangdang's listing on the NYSE, JD.com escalated the competition by announcing a 20 percent price cut across all its books benchmarked to Dangdang's prices. Dangdang responded swiftly, lowering its prices further and offering a similar 100 yuan off when spending 200 yuan promotion. Not to be left behind, Amazon China joined the fray the following day, also cutting prices by 20 percent.

This unprecedented price war provoked widespread protests from publishers and brick-and-mortar bookstores and eventually prompted intervention by the NPPA, which ordered the three companies to halt their aggressive discounting and revert to earlier prices. Despite this, price wars persisted in the following years, driving significant changes in the dynamic of the online bookselling market. Where previously, the typical discount offered by online bookstores fell within the range of 15 percent to 28 percent, by 2019, this had risen to an average of 41 percent, compared to just 11 percent in physical bookstores, according to OpenBook.[24] This stark disparity created great challenges for physical bookstores to compete with online retailers.

This shift in the retail space also affected publishers, who faced mounting pressures from the likes of JD and Dangdang to give deeper discounts. That is, to offset losses from selling books at extremely low prices, these large online bookstores demanded higher discounts from publishers, which created considerable financial strains for the latter. To cope with this, many publishers resorted to the strategy of upping book prices. By increasing list prices, they could accommodate the platforms' demands for higher discounts while still maintaining reasonable profit margins. OpenBook's data suggest that although the median book price in China has been steadily increasing since 1999, it rose particularly sharply in the 2010s, going up from just over 30 yuan in 2012 to 45 yuan in 2019, a 50 percent increase in just seven years.[25]

Tmall Books, on the other hand, brought about another key change to the Chinese book retailing industry: More publishers, distributors, and wholesalers have embraced the platform and opened their own online Tmall stores to directly engage with consumers. Leveraging Alibaba's vast ecosystem—with 891 million monthly active users as of March 2021—and its world-class e-commerce and digital payment infrastructure, Tmall Books became the platform of choice for publishers who wished to establish their own online bookstores.[26] By 2016, Tmall Books had attracted over four hundred publishers, encompassing both state-owned publishing houses and privately owned book companies.[27] The figure is bound to be even larger today. Not only publishers but also many local book wholesalers and regional distributors turned to Tmall Books to expand their reach. During a visit to a large book wholesale center in Beijing in 2014, I discovered that more than half of the wholesalers trading there were also selling books on Tmall Books. Conversations with several wholesalers revealed that some of them were selling more books on Tmall than in their physical stores. Tmall's rise thus has changed not only the retail sector but also the distribution and wholesaling ecosystems in the Chinese book industry.

THE RISE OF INDEPENDENT BOOKSTORES

Beginning in the early to mid-2000s, some practitioners and observers in the Chinese book business began to use the term *duli shudian*, or "independent bookstore," to refer to a specific type of bookstore in China. While it is difficult to pinpoint the precise origin of the term or identify its first user, it is evident that by the 2010s, the concept had gained widespread usage in the Chinese book trade. It was commonly used to refer to a particular kind of bookstore considered different from both state-owned Xinhua Bookstores and conventional privately owned bookstores. The growing popularity of this concept and the bookstores it designated was evidenced by the publication of several trade books that introduced and celebrated these independent bookstores in the early 2010s. Figure 1.8 shows the covers of two such books: *Hello, The Independent Bookstore* (left), published in 2011, which tells stories about twenty-seven independent bookstores in twenty-five Chinese cities, and *A Roaming Guide to Chinese Independent Bookstores* (right), published in 2013, which introduces eighty-six independent bookstores in twenty-three provinces. In addition to these publications, the growing influence of independent bookstores was evidenced by a series of trade meetings on this topic held during the 2010s. For example, the Beijing Book Fair hosted two plenary sessions in 2012 and 2013 that were dedicated to discussing this development.

Liu Suli, a prominent bookseller and the founder-owner of a famous scholarly bookstore established in the 1990s in Beijing, considers himself an early adopter of the term "independent bookstore" in China. During an interview, he recalled that as early as 2004, he began to describe his bookstore as an independent bookstore rather than a scholarly bookstore. "Over time,"

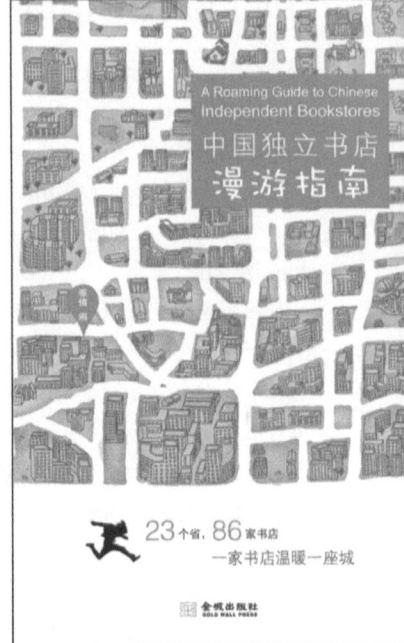

FIGURE 1.8 The covers of two books on independent bookstores in China
Source: Xue Yuan and Yang Hongyu; Guo Yaqian

he said, "more and more people started to call these 'scholarly bookstores' *duli shudian*."

The rest of the 2010s witnessed a rapid increase in the number of independent bookstores. During my initial fieldwork in 2014, I had no difficulty finding bookstore owners or managers who classified their bookstores as *duli shudian* and were willing to participate in my interviews. Remarkably, all these individuals seemed to share a consensus regarding the meaning and scope of the term *duli shudian* despite its relatively recent emergence in the Chinese book trade. In spite of this growth, however, there has never been any official attempt to quantify the number of independent bookstores in China. Estimations have to rely on educated guesses and "a sense of the trade." In 2014, I was invited to join a WeChat group created by the author of *A Roaming Guide to Chinese Independent Bookstores* for independent bookstore owners or managers nationwide. This group, which remains the largest online community of independent booksellers in China, had approximately one hundred members when I first joined in 2014. By March 2024, it had grown to just under five hundred members and had led to the creation of a sister group of a similar size to comply with WeChat's member limit for individual groups (maximum five hundred members per group). While this WeChat community cannot encompass all of China's independent bookstores, its expansion over the past decade serves as a valuable indicator of the field's growth over the years.

In the next chapter, I delve into the world of independent bookstores, comparing the differing definitions of the term "independent bookstore" in the Chinese and Western book industries and drawing a detailed account of how China's independent booksellers understand and construct their independent identity.

2

SEARCHING FOR AN INDEPENDENT IDENTITY

In this chapter, I examine the defining features of independent bookstores in China. This analysis is juxtaposed with an examination of the concept's meaning and scope in the West, especially in the UK and US book trades. By comparing the differing approaches adopted by Chinese and Western independent booksellers to defining and attaining an independent identity, I uncover key differences in the underlying dynamics shaping bookselling and book cultures in these contrasting contexts. I argue that the development of the book business in the United Kingdom and the United States is primarily shaped by an interplay between commercial forces and cultural interests. In contrast, the Chinese book industry operates within a framework that includes an additional political dimension. The interactions between cultural, economic, and political forces and factors profoundly shape not only the rise of independent bookstores but also other major developments in the Chinese book industry.

INDEPENDENT BOOKSELLING IN THE WEST

The concept of "independent bookstore" is relatively easier to define and picture in the Western context, for in countries like the United Kingdom and the United States, an independent bookstore is simply understood to be a nonchain bookstore. In these countries, physical book retailing is typically dominated by three major types of players: large national bookselling chains (e.g., Waterstones in the United Kingdom and Barnes & Noble in the United States), supermarkets, and independent bookstores. Among these, only the chains and independent bookstores are considered professional booksellers, which naturally leads to a juxtaposition between them that highlights their different roles, approaches, and practices in bookselling. As Laura Miller notes in her authoritative book on the evolution of the US bookselling industry, it was not until the rise of chain bookstores in the 1960s and 1970s that the term "independent bookstore" became a meaningful and widely used concept. That is, it was the advent of chains that catalyzed the crystallization and wider acceptance of the notion of independent bookstores in the US book trade. According to Miller, prior to the chain's emergence, the term "personal bookseller" was more commonly used to describe the small, individually run bookstores, which later came to be known as "independent bookstores." The word *personal* aptly captures the essence of these establishments. Owned and managed by individual proprietors rather than by large corporations, these bookshops prioritized cultivating personal relationships with their patrons. Such personal touch became a defining feature, setting them apart from department stores and nonbook retailers at the time and from chain bookstores that emerged later.[1]

From the 1960s, mall-based bookstores began to proliferate. They differed from the traditional personal bookstores for being highly uniform in appearance and centrally managed by distant headquarters. These organizational features earned them the label "chain bookstores." The term *chain* highlighted not only these bookstores' ownership structure but also an important operational trait: a high degree of standardization and efficiency. For Miller, it was this operational trait that fundamentally differentiated chain bookstores from personal bookstores and, later, from independent bookstores.

The rise of chain bookstores greatly disrupted the business of personal bookstores. It pushed them to adapt to the new bookselling culture by adopting some practices popularized by the chains, such as widening and diversifying their book offerings to attract a broader range of customers beyond the educated, upper-middle class and creating more inviting store environments. Moreover, personal bookstores began to collaborate in their battle with the chains. In this process, forging a unified identity to distinguish them from the chain bookstores emerged as a key strategy. Central to this new identity was the narrative that being small and individually run operations gave these personal bookstores a unique charm that chain bookstores could not mimic. This charm thus afforded them a competitive advantage. Furthermore, their autonomy, especially their ability to make decisions independently of any corporate headquarters, also distinguished them from the chains, forming the second crucial dimension of this newly crafted identity: the *independent* identity.

Viewed from this historical perspective, it is clear that the evolution of the concept of independent bookstore in the Western book trade has always been closely linked to the development of chain bookstores, so much so that, oftentimes, independent bookstores are simply understood in opposition to what chains represent. For example, during the last two decades of the twentieth century, as chain bookstores increasingly boasted a national presence, independent bookstores began to accentuate and celebrate their local roots and relevance. They were—and continue to be—widely regarded as establishments committed to serving local communities and celebrating local cultures. Recognizing this distinction, Miller identifies "being locally based" and "limited in geographic scope" as a central theme of the independent identity, alongside "smallness." Similarly, as chain bookstores—including book superstores—became more and more standardized and commercialized, independent bookstores emphasized their commitment to cultural values over commercial interests to effectively differentiate themselves from the commercially driven chain bookstores.[2]

Today, a cultural commitment, local focus, and noncorporate ownership are the three key defining features of independent bookstores in the Western book business. Although a hybrid bookstore type, called "independent chain," has emerged in recent years, which appears to blur the boundaries between the independent and the chain, as Miller argues, this is not a new type of bookstore. Instead, this oxymoron serves to highlight how the concept of independent bookstore is evolving to encompass a wider range of novel bookselling practices and innovative organizational structures adopted by some independent bookstores as they continue to adapt to the changing bookselling culture. Miller hence argues that the independent identity today is increasingly defined and signified by a "state of mind" and set of values rather than organizational features, such as the size of a bookstore.[3] In other words, the term "independent bookstore" has evolved into a highly value-laden concept, placing a greater emphasis on the ethos and principles that define what it means to be independent rather than specific organizational or operational traits.

In the remainder of this chapter, I give a detailed description and analysis of the meaning and scope of "independent bookstore," or *duli shudian*, in China. I argue that while sharing some common assumptions with its Western usage, *duli shudian* represents a distinctly differing approach to book retailing, reflecting unique practices and perspectives developed in the Chinese context.

OWNERSHIP STRUCTURE

The independent bookstore owners or managers I interviewed all referred to nonstate ownership as the first criterion for defining the independent bookstore identity. As noted in chapter 1, the Chinese bookselling industry has traditionally been dominated by two major types of book retailers: the state-owned Xinhua Bookstore and the privately owned bookstore. The criterion of nonstate ownership, therefore, serves to distinguish independent bookstores from the state-owned Xinhua Bookstore. However, it also reflects another consideration important to independent bookstores: their desire to retain a high degree of economic and cultural autonomy through private ownership. For many of the independent booksellers I spoke to, being SOEs (state owned enterprises), Xinhua Bookstores are perceived as having limited operational autonomy compared to privately owned bookstores, especially in areas such as book selection. As mentioned previously, most Xinhua Bookstore retail branches have little discretion over inventory selection, for stock is normally centrally allocated to them by their head stores. Many independent booksellers quoted this lack of discretion and autonomy as a key reason why Xinhua Bookstores cannot be considered independent and that the independent identity necessitates private ownership and operational autonomy.

The criterion of nonstate ownership may seem self-evident: the term *independent* is almost intrinsically incompatible with state ownership. However, if the underlying rationale here is simply an emphasis on a bookstore's financial discretion and operational autonomy, then aspiring independent bookstores should avoid corporate ownership just as much as state ownership. Yet opinions among the independent booksellers I interviewed divided significantly on the implications of corporate ownership for a bookstore's independent status. Notably, a clear disagreement arose between those believing that independent bookstores should be strictly individually owned and run businesses and those in favor of corporate involvement in independent bookstores, whether through ownership or investment.

In order to understand the full spectrum of perspectives, I recruited interview participants from both individually run bookstores and bookstores owned by large corporations, as well as bookstores that had received venture capital (VC) investment. All interviewees identified their bookstores as *duli shudian*. Unsurprisingly, their opinions aligned precisely with their bookstores' ownership structures. Specifically, managers of corporation-owned independent bookstores often stressed their nonstate ownership as the defining factor of their independent status. Similarly, managers of VC-funded independent bookstores tended to emphasize two points: the nonstate ownership of their investors and their own cultural commitment. In contrast, proprietors of individually owned independent bookstores often questioned the independent status of corporation-owned or VC-funded bookstores. They contended that the inescapable influence of corporate owners or investors is bound to restrict these bookstores' ability to maintain full autonomy, posing a challenge to their true independence. The following quotations illustrate these contrasting perspectives.

Explaining why he believed that independent bookstores should never accept external investments, especially from professional investors such as venture capitalists, the owner of a small but thriving independent bookstore stated: "Once you accept the investor's money, they will turn you into their money-making machine and make you to go down the commercial route to maximize their capital gains."

Reflecting upon whether corporate ownership can be interoperable with the independent identity, the managing director of a large corporation-owned independent bookstore, who was formerly the owner of a small individually run bookstore, remarked:

> I don't feel I am now less free than when I was running my own business. My boss, the founder and chairman of the parent company, gives me full support and autonomy to run this bookstore as I wish. If anything, I feel I now have more freedom to do what I want to do with this bookstore than I previously did with my own bookstore because now I have the money to do the things I want to do. Previously, I was so financially constrained that I sometimes had to sell books I didn't want to sell, but I had to sell them to make more money. Nowadays, I no longer have that kind of constraint and can concentrate on selecting and selling the best books. I think this is an improvement.

When asked how they balanced their personal cultural commitment with the parent company's profit expectations, this manager explained: "Achieving profitability is as important to smaller independent bookstores as it is to us. A bookstore isn't more independent by ignoring the finances. Many independent booksellers are against capital and capital operation, seeing them as incompatible with the book business.[4] I disagree. I think capital is a good thing: it has allowed me to better pursue my cultural goals by giving me more financial latitude."

How should we interpret these statements? Are they the genuine views of this interviewee—a salaried managing director of a large, corporation-run bookstore that had never turned a profit since its establishment—or should they be taken with a pinch of salt? In my view, these statements are authentic and credible. This is not least because this bookstore—at the time of the interview—held an inventory consisting almost exclusively of high-quality intellectual, literary, and artistic titles, a testament to the manager's claim that cultural excellence is the sole criterion for book selection in this store. Moreover, as this manager emphasized, having a parent company not only did not hinder the bookstore's pursuit of cultural goals but was essential to it in that the financial backing from the parent company enabled the management team to focus on providing the best books without having to constantly worry about sales and profits. To underscore this point, this manager even recounted to me how the owner of the parent company assured them when making the appointment that achieving profitability was not "a short-term goal" the parent company had for this bookstore.

While this may sound like a perfect offer to any bookseller—being able to curate the best books without the pressure of turning a profit—it comes with an implicit condition: The bookstore must generate other forms of benefit to the parent company. As will be explored in more detail in chapter 5, the rationale for nonbook corporations' investment in independent bookselling is often tied to marketing and business expansion purposes. That is, the corporation-funded independent bookstores are often expected to add a desired sense of cultural prestige to the parent company's branding or serve as a springboard for the parent company to explore new business opportunities in the broader cultural and creative industries. All of these have been cited by the independent booksellers I interviewed from both individually run and corporation-owned bookstores as motivations driving nonbook corporations' investment in independent bookselling.

Regardless of the specific motivations, such investment is ultimately aimed at attaining long-term returns rather than short-term profits made from bookselling. This dynamic, however, can be risky to the independent bookstores concerned. If they fail to deliver on the parent company's long-term goals, they risk losing both financial support and cultural autonomy. Acknowledging this risk, this manager added, "Long-term wise, we must find a way to make blood ourselves [be self-sufficient]." They went on to explain how, since the bookshop's opening, they had added a coffee shop, a venue hire business, and an extensive line of nonbook merchandise to help generate more revenue.

Diversifying into profitable nonbook business lines is a popular strategy China's independent bookstores adopt to compensate for losses from bookselling. However, when discussing these initiatives, many independent booksellers felt compelled to disassociate their independent identity from these profit-driven activities. They emphasized that their independence was warranted by and rooted in their dedication to providing high-quality books, a course of action they viewed as separate from profit-maximizing activities such as selling nonbook merchandise. This careful demarcation between their commitment to providing high-quality books, often taking a loss, and engagement in profit-oriented nonbook ventures marks independent bookstores' unique approach to balancing between cultural distinction and economic viability.

Venture capitalists investing in independent bookstores operate under a different set of motivations. Generally speaking, bookselling is not the kind of business that would typically draw the attention of venture capitalists. Venture capital (VC) is more interested in startup businesses with the potential for rapid and substantial growth, which is why VC investments tend to concentrate on high-tech sectors. By contrast, bookselling, known for its low profit margins and sluggish growth, rarely appeals to venture capitalists. For this reason, I was surprised to discover that one of the independent bookstores I studied had indeed received a large venture capital investment, and I was curious to find out how this investment might affect the bookstore's approach to bookselling and its independent identity.

Before delving into this particular case, it is helpful to first consider how accepting VC funding can change an organization. Generally speaking, VC investment can change a company in two major ways. First, it can change its decision-making process. By acquiring an equity stake, venture capitalists can often secure positions on the invested company's board and, hence, gain a voice in critical business decisions. It is also common for venture capitalists or their representatives to take on senior management roles within the invested company. While this practice can be beneficial to the invested company—for example, by providing crucial managerial expertise that may be lacking in the founding team—it also allows the venture capitalists to directly influence the firm's decision-making. Hence, an important consequence for organizations accepting VC funding is the trade-off between securing the much-need capital for growth and the partial loss of autonomy to their investors. Second, VC will drive the invested company to grow and scale up quickly. VC operates by acquiring early-stage companies, increasing their market value, and then divesting once valuations rise. Because VC funds, normally sourced from limited partners, must liquidate within fixed timeframes (usually three to seven years in China), fund managers face great pressure to expedite the invested company's growth. Incremental but modest progress is insufficient, as they seek swift and substantial expansion. As a result, VC-backed companies often find themselves undergoing a frenetic period of opening new stores, entering new markets, launching new products or services, and hiring aggressively, all to achieve quick and substantial growth within the limited fund lifespan.

With an understanding of how VC works, we can now consider how VC investment might affect an independent bookstore's operations. First, it is reasonable to infer that accepting VC investment will reduce a bookstore's capacity to act on its own terms. Recognizing this, when asked about their investor's influence, the cofounder of a VC-funded independent bookstore did not deny its existence. Instead, they justified the store's independence by stressing the alignment of the founding team's goals and those of the investor. This cofounder remarked:

> I know that many people are saying that we will change now that we have an investor, but that is not true. We are still an independent bookstore and will always be. For me, accepting external investments does not mean giving up our independence. We remain independent because our investor, like us, is a non-state-owned business entity. The money doesn't come from the government, so it does not compromise our independent identity.... You asked whether the investor will try to influence us. Yes, they have their ideas of how the bookstore should be run, but what I can tell you is that their ideas align with ours. They share our commitment to selling high-quality books, and that's why we chose them as our investor in the first place.

Two points are worth noting here. First, for this cofounder, the only intrinsic factor that would automatically negate a bookstore's independent status is a financial relationship with a state entity. Financial relationships with external entities—be it a venture capital firm or a corporate parent company—do not compromise a bookstore's independence, provided that these entities are also nonstate-owned. Further emphasizing this point in response to a follow-up question, this cofounder added: "We raised the capital through the market, not from the government, so it doesn't change our status as an independent bookstore." Second, this interviewee offered an intriguing perspective on reconciling a bookstore's independent identity with having an external investor capable of exerting influence. For this cofounder, the key lies in the bookstore's *voluntary acceptance* of the investor's influence. By embracing the investor's goals and aligning them with their own objectives, the bookstore effectively integrates the investor's influence, thereby removing its externality. In this way, the influence is no longer perceived as externally imposed but as harmonized with the bookstore's own initiatives. Through this strategic alignment, the bookstore conforms to an *internalist* interpretation of the independent identity, which equates independence with freedom from external control. This perspective is particularly popular among owner-managers of individually run independent bookstores, who consider autonomy from external control a core measure of independent standing. Therefore, by willingly accepting their investor's influence, and so reframing it as nonexternal, this cofounder cleverly justifies this relationship, thereby sustaining their bookstore's claim to independence.

The reader can judge the persuasiveness of this justification for themselves. For me, the justification is unnecessary, and this cofounder's urge to rationalize their acceptance of the investor's influence appears to manifest their inner discomfort with it. The justification is redundant because an investor holding a significant stake in a company naturally has the right to participate in its decision-making. Framing this involvement as something needing defense seems needless. From this perspective, we can argue that the debate over the role of external investors in independent bookstores is less about how exactly the investor interacts with the bookstore—some may well indeed take a hands-off approach and let the bookstore do their own things—and more about the symbolic ramifications of having a corporate owner-investor for organizations claiming the title of independence and autonomy. Critics of VC-funded independent bookstores are not opposed to the specific actions of the investors; rather, their concern lies more in the nature of these entities: Venture capital firms, as embodiments of commercialism and profit-driven motives, are perceived as intrinsically incongruent with the culture-oriented ethos of independent bookselling. This sentiment mirrors the "independent vs. chain" dichotomy that defines the independent bookstore in the Western context. As Miller argues, independent bookstores in the United States are not so much against capitalism as they are opposed to the excessive commercialism corrupting the book trade.[5] While Chinese independent bookstores differ in some key aspects from their Western counterparts, their debates surrounding VC investors and corporate owners reflect their shared concern over the growing encroachment of commercialism in the realm of book retailing.

This section does not aim to provide a fixed definition of independent bookstores based on ownership structure. Instead, it seeks to explore how independent booksellers in China perceive and construct their independent identity with regard to organizational ownership. While some ideas discussed here garnered broad consensus among the booksellers I interviewed, others sparked heated debate. This diversity of perspectives highlights the challenge of establishing a single, clear-cut criterion for defining independent bookstores in terms of ownership. Meanwhile, it is important to recognize that any bookstore can self-identify as an independent bookstore without needing external validation. As this chapter's title suggests, the independent identity is an aspiration, a construct actively pursued rather than a status conferred to a bookstore. That is, it is a conscious choice, not an externally validated recognition. While debates about the meaning and scope of the independent identity are inevitable, it is neither possible nor meaningful to strip away this identity from a bookstore that proclaims it.

Consider the case of the aforementioned VC-backed bookstore. An anecdote shared with me by another interviewee about this bookstore is revealing. It is about an incident where this VC-backed bookstore had to cancel an event due to pressure from its investor. This interviewee recounted: "We had an author event earlier this year. It was initially planned to take place at xx [the VC-backed bookstore]. But they cancelled it at the last minute because their investor thought the author was a bit politically controversial and hence asked them to call it off. So the publisher moved the event to us, and it was all right—no one [from the government] asked any questions. So what's interesting about this was that it was in fact their investor, not the government, that got them to cancel the event."

This anecdote challenges the VC-backed bookstore's claim to be autonomous from its investor, especially the cofounder's assertion of their aligned goals. It suggests, instead, that the investor held considerable power over the bookstore's operations, including an ability to override the management's decisions. In this light, the alignment of goals portrayed by the cofounder appears overstated.

However, rather than interpreting this incongruity as dishonesty on the part of the cofounder interviewed, it is more constructive to see it as evidence of the inherently cognitively constructed nature of the independent identity. As a cognitive construct rather than a fixed, quantifiable trait, the independent identity by nature resists clear-cut definitions or qualifications. Bookstores need not prove their independence to claim it, for this identity exists through their adoption and enactment of it. Such identity—and the prestige surrounding it—will cease to exist when bookstores no longer value or uphold it. From this standpoint, it is important to examine not only how the concept of independent bookstore is defined in the Chinese context but also why Chinese independent booksellers construe and construct this identity as they do. Comprehending this can shed critical light on the social, cultural, and economic relationships that shape independent bookselling as well as the broader cultural production processes and practices in China.

One such key relationship, for instance, is the shared desire of independent booksellers to reinstate culture's central and autonomous role in cultural production. It can be said that the evolution of China's cultural industries since 1949 has been driven by the interplay between political demands and economic imperatives. Prior to the 2000s, cultural production was dominated by state-funded entities serving public and political functions. The corporatization reforms of the 2000s and 2010s shifted this landscape, elevating the market as another steering force. Throughout these changes, however, the cultural dimension has constantly been overshadowed by political and economic priorities. A comment made by President Xi Jinping in a speech about the cultural industries illustrates this dynamic: "The cultural industries have both an ideological attribute and a market attribute, with the ideological attribute being the fundamental attribute."[6] Notably absent from this characterization is any mention of culture as an intrinsic value of cultural production.

The marginalization of the cultural dimension in cultural production can be said to have driven independent bookstores' striving for an independent identity that emphasizes autonomy from both political and economic influences. However, while they share a common approach to limiting political influence—by being strictly privately owned entities—independent bookstores differ in their attitudes toward the market and commercial forces. Recognizing that market forces can both enable and constrain cultural production, some independent bookstores choose to distance themselves from both political and commercial influences, while others choose to capitalize on market opportunities. This division forms a core dynamic driving the development of independent bookstores and is a key to understanding their practices.

OPERATIONS

The second defining feature of independent bookstores concerns the number of stores they can operate. Opinions diverge between those holding that true independence requires maintaining a single-store operation and those contending that running multiple outlets does not contradict the independent status. For the latter, a bookstore can preserve its independent identity while managing a chain of outlets to maximize sales and profits. On the surface, this debate appears to be regarding the scale and operational strategies of independent bookstores. Fundamentally, however, it is concerned with the relationship between independent bookselling and commercialism and commercialization. While some deem profit maximization through commercialization as inherently at odds with the very idea of independent bookselling, others see it as an innocent practical management choice, separate from the value aspect of the independent narrative.

The Debate

Unsurprisingly, owners of small, individually run bookstores were the main advocates of the notion that independent bookstores should be single-store operations. They argue that running multiple branches contradicts the independent identity. As one owner of such a bookstore noted: "An independent bookstore should be small enough, fine enough, and artistic enough [*zugou xiao, zugou jing, zugou mei*] to distinguish itself from other bookstores. The word *independence* implies uniqueness, and uniqueness requires that there be only one such store in the world which cannot be replicated." For this bookseller and others with similar views, independent bookstores are akin to boutique stores: small, exquisitely curated, and exuding a unique charm. Since these qualities are difficult to replicate or sustain without losing authenticity and uniqueness, independent bookstores, by nature, resist standardization and replication, making single-store operations the only viable choice for bookstores claiming this title.

Another interviewee offered a slightly different perspective. Also the owner of a small, single-store independent bookshop, they stated: "There are good independent bookstores and bad independent bookstores. . . . Being an independent bookstore does not necessarily mean that it's a *good* bookstore. It only means that the bookstore has some unique features that distinguish it from other bookstores. A bad but unique bookstore can still be an independent bookstore. But a nice-looking chain bookstore is not an independent." When asked what a "bad" independent bookstore might look like, they said: "Perhaps the books it sells aren't of great quality. However, if the books are selected by the owner based on their personal tastes and preferences, then the bookstore is still unique because it reflects the owner's personal views and ideas. . . . When we talk about independent bookstores, we don't talk about their 'taste' as such. A bookstore needs not to have the finest taste to qualify as an independent. Rather, we talk about whether a bookstore has its own unique ideas and attitude." Unlike the first interviewee, this bookseller did not consider cultural sophistication a key to an independent identity. Instead, they see uniqueness as more relevant to it. For them, uniqueness does not equate to or necessarily imply cultural sophistication but merely signifies individuality or even idiosyncrasy. This uniqueness arises from the shop owner's application of their personal value systems to the operations of their bookstore, from book selection to store design to customer service. In other words, this interpretation of independence centers on the distinctive and personal imprint the owner leaves on their bookstore rather than on any external standard like cultural sophistication.

Despite their differing views on the origins of uniqueness in independent bookstores—cultural sophistication versus individuality—both interviewees agreed that independence is defined by uniqueness and distinctiveness. They also both linked this uniqueness to small-scale operations, considering both cultural sophistication and individuality as best expressed and realized in smaller stores, as opposed to chains. In this way, both perspectives support the single-store model as the most appropriate operational model for independent bookstores.

Opposing viewpoints were expressed by booksellers from large, multistore independent bookstores. These individuals reject the notion that independence is tied to a bookstore's size and instead argue that what defines independence is the bookstore's value orientation. As the managing director of a four-store independent bookshop remarked: "Being independent and running multiple branches are separate matters. Independence is concerned with a bookstore's value orientation, not the number of branches it owns. Not all single-store bookstores are independent, so conversely, an independent bookstore can run more than one branch so long as it upholds its independent values across all branches." Another bookseller echoed this view by stressing the practical need for multistore operations for some independent bookstores: "Our cities are so large that running several stores is sometimes essential to serving customers. For example, Beijing's Chaoyang District alone is larger than many European cities. So to reach my customers, I need more than one store. But this doesn't mean that I prioritize profit over culture. We are still committed to providing the best quality books, and this is what makes us an independent bookstore."

These viewpoints were shared by many other independent booksellers I interviewed. Deep down, they reflect a widely held perspective on the relationship between culture and commercialism in independent bookstores. This perspective asserts that cultural goals and commercial objectives should and can be pursued separately, each guided by different principles and approaches. Within this framework, the question of independence is considered a cultural concern, while multistore operations are framed as a practical management choice, allowing them to be argued as disparate matters with minimal influence over one another. By framing the question of independence as a cultural matter with limited impact on operation choices and vice versa, this strategic framing avoids the controversial question of whether a bookstore can maintain its independent ethos while simultaneously embracing a commercially driven approach to bookselling.

However, not everyone accepts this line of reasoning. Several interviewees challenged the notion of reducing operational choices as mere practical management decisions and instead argued that the independent identity prescribes certain operational practices, including the single-store operational model. As the owner of a small yet highly popular independent bookstore in Beijing explained: "I didn't open this bookshop to make money. For me, it's not about running a business, but about pursuing a personal passion [*zhuiqiu geren xingqu*]. So if my goal isn't about making more money, why would I need so many stores?" For this interviewee, operating multiple branches is an active choice driven by profit-maximization motives rather than a management necessity. Another owner of a small independent bookstore echoed this sentiment: "Independent bookstores should only be those founded by their owners to pursue a personal passion for books without the slightest concern for economic returns [*meiyou yisi dui jingji huibao de suqiu*].... Ultimately, it's a question of whether you run the bookstore for personal enthusiasm [*geren aihao*] or for profits." Once again, multistore operations are cast as a profit-oriented initiative, which is inherently incompatible with the independent value. A counterpoint was made by the above-quoted bookseller, who stressed the practical necessity of multistore operations. They reasoned: "I always tell my colleagues that at xx [this bookstore's name], we strive to balance cultural and commercial goals without sacrificing one for the other—whether that means sacrificing culture for commerce or vice versa. Therefore, I do not reject commercialism; I think commercialization is crucial for our survival. I believe that as long as the bookstore's owner maintains an independent spirit, the bookstore remains independent, even if it uses commercial methods to generate more income."

The debate around the relationship between culture and commerce in independent bookstores can be better understood through Pierre Bourdieu's theory of two types of cultural production. Bourdieu distinguishes between a restricted mode of cultural production—where cultural goods are produced on a small scale to maintain cultural standards—and a large-scale mode of cultural production, where cultural goods target mass markets to maximize economic returns.[7] These models fundamentally differ in how they prioritize cultural and commercial considerations: the restricted mode places cultural quality first, while the large-scale mode emphasizes economic gain. Applying this framework, we can understand the single-store advocates as embracing a culture-centric approach to independent bookselling, prioritizing cultural standards over profit. By contrast, those favoring multistore operations accept commercial strategies as a means to try to achieve cultural and economic objectives simultaneously. In the following chapters, I will explore how this debate over the relationship between culture and commerce has shaped many other key aspects of independent bookstores and their practices.

ETHOS

The final major criterion for defining independent bookstores concerns the independent ethos. Two closely linked elements stand out to be particularly relevant: individuality and an independent spirit. Although interconnected, these dimensions manifest differently and influence the behaviors of independent bookstores in different ways.

Apart from the criterion of nonstate ownership, the second most widely cited criterion for independent bookstores is having individuality, or *you gexing* in Chinese. "You must have unique individuality [*dute de gexing*] to become an independent bookstore," said one interviewee who owned and ran a small independent bookshop in Beijing. Another bookstore owner from the same city similarly remarked: "In my opinion, the most important quality for independent bookstores to have is personality. Others might define independence in terms of political independence or economic independence, but for me, independence is all about having a unique character that distinguishes the bookstore from other bookstores." They continued, "My independence lies in how I select books, arrange and display them, and design and decorate my shop. I make all these decisions based on my own ideas and thoughts, and this is what makes me an 'independent' bookseller." Such sentiments were very common among those I interviewed, highlighting individuality as one widely agreed on key component of the independent identity.

The Cambridge Dictionary defines *individuality* as "the qualities that make a person or thing different from others."[8] Similarly, the Chinese term *you gexing* (having individuality) denotes that a person or entity possesses qualities that distinguish them from others. Therefore, the first element of the independent ethos—possessing individuality—implies that an independent bookstore should exhibit distinct traits that set it apart not only from nonindependent bookstores but also from other independent bookstores. In other words, it must be recognizably unique. This emphasis on distinctiveness is specific to the Chinese understanding of "independent bookstore" and is not found in the Western definition of this notion.

Several interviewees accentuated the importance of individuality by contrasting it with other qualities often associated with the independent identity, such as cultural sophistication and intellectual excellence. As one bookseller put it: "A bookstore needs not to be intellectually sophisticated [*you sixiang*] to be independent, but it must have individuality. . . . It's fine if it doesn't have an impeccable taste for books, for what makes a bookstore independent isn't its intellectual depth [*sixiang xing*] but individuality. Not all independent bookstores have to be like Wansheng. What really matters is whether the bookstore owner exercises their personal judgement when selecting books or just follow others." Wansheng is a famous independent bookstore in Beijing known for its high-quality book selection and widely regarded as an exemplary independent bookstore in China. Yet this interviewee contended that cultural and intellectual depth are not a defining benchmark for independence. Instead, uniqueness and individuality are more important. This quotation also highlights the origin of individuality: the owner's personal input into their bookstore. As another interviewee succinctly put it: "An independent bookstore is a place where you can feel the owner's idiosyncrasies. If you can't feel the owners' presence in the bookstore, then it is soulless and is not an independent bookstore."

This emphasis on the bookstore owner's personal imprint is echoed in the Western understanding of independent bookstores. Miller, for instance, underscores that acting idiosyncratically is a key feature of US independent bookstores. However, the meaning of *idiosyncrasy* seems to differ between the Western and Chinese contexts. In Miller's account, idiosyncrasy stands in opposition to "a single-minded focus on profit"; to act idiosyncratically thus means to act "according to criteria that are not always economic in nature."[9] As a result, describing a Western independent bookstore as idiosyncratic primarily implies it follows a culture-centric, rather than a profit-driven, approach to bookselling. In contrast, Chinese independent booksellers interpret idiosyncrasy in terms of differentiation and distinctiveness—seeking to stand out from others rather than just prioritizing culture over profit.

The Chinese term for "independent," *duli* (独立), conveys a nuanced sense of standing out and being noticeable, a connotation absent in the English word *independent*. In English, *independent* generally signifies two main ideas: autonomy from external control and self-sufficiency. In contrast, *duli* carries richer meanings, which may be the source of Chinese independent bookstores' emphasis on distinguishability and recognizability. This particular connotation of *duli* is vividly illustrated in a famous poem from the Han dynasty, which was composed more than two thousand years ago to celebrate a woman's resplendent beauty. The poem reads as follows:

李延年歌 (Li Yannian Ge)
Song of Li Yannian
北方有佳人 (Beifang you jiaren),
There is a beauty in the northern lands,
绝世而独立 (Jueshi er **duli**).
Unequaled, **high above the world she stands**.
一顾倾人城 (Yigu qing rencheng),
At her first sight, soldiers would lose their town,
再顾倾人国 (Zaigu qing renguo).
At her second, a monarch would his crown.

As we can see, the translator does not translate *duli* into "independent." Instead, he uses the phrase "high above the world she stands" to capture the original context's emphasis on the lady's extraordinary, unmatched beauty.[10] This sense of standing out and being noticeable is integral to the Chinese notion of *duli* and is a main source of Chinese independent booksellers' emphasis on differentiation as a key element of their independent identity. This longing for distinction also sets Chinese independent bookstores apart from their counterparts operating in different socio-cultural contexts.

The German sociologist Niklas Luhmann argues that the meaning of something is defined by what it is not.[11] From this perspective, independent bookstores establish their identity through the differences they assert. The question, then, is: From whom or what do these independent bookstores seek to differentiate themselves? I argue that they primarily strive to distinguish themselves from the state-owned Xinhua Bookstore. Although some interviewees also mentioned distinguishing themselves from nonindependent privately owned bookstores, most discussions on the independent ethos centered around the need to stand out from the state-owned bookseller by demonstrating individuality.

Independent booksellers regard individuality as an effective means of distinguishing themselves from Xinhua Bookstores in that the latter has long been seen as uniform and lacking character. As discussed in chapter 1, Xinhua's unique role in the Chinese bookselling field—as a kind of "display window" for publishers—limits local Xinhua Bookstores' latitude in book selection and leaves them with little room for aesthetic tailoring and enhancement. Consequently, although most Xinhua Bookstores are very well-stocked, their inventory often lacks careful curation. This led many independent booksellers I interviewed to criticize Xinhua for "selling everything" and lacking cultural discrimination. Therefore, by emphasizing their own individuality, these bookstores seek to highlight their difference from this industry leader. In doing so, they also assert their distance from the state itself. Here, the focus on individuality resonates and aligns with the principle of nonstate ownership, which once again manifests independent bookstores' deep-seated desire to restore and retain culture's central and autonomous role in the Chinese cultural sphere.

In contrast to the criterion of demonstrating individuality, the criterion of having an independent spirit may initially appear redundant: Shouldn't such a spirit be something intrinsic to any bookstore claiming to be independent? The reason why some, though not all, independent booksellers I interviewed emphasized this quality pertains to, once again, their strong desire to differentiate themselves from state players in China's bookselling and cultural sphere by offering alternative voices and perspectives.

As one interviewee explained: "Ultimately, a bookstore's independence lies in whether its owner possesses an independent attitude toward books and culture, and if they can express their independent attitude via the books they sell. . . . Being independent is a little like being antimainstream [*fan zhuliu*]: you must have your own independent thoughts [*duli de sixiang*] and are unafraid to express them in order to be called an independent bookseller." Another bookseller made a similar comment: "Apart from financial independence, what matters is the owner's ability to think and act independently. Only with this ability can they choose books that reflect their individual stances and tastes, and create a bookstore different from others." Viewed from these perspectives, the independent spirit, as understood by these booksellers, entails a high degree of nonconformity, making alternative-seeking another key feature of some, though not all, independent bookstores in China.[12]

3

CULTURALLY ADAPTED STRATEGIES: THE CONCEPT

This chapter introduces the reader to the concept of the culturally adapted strategy as a key framework to critically understand the practices of independent bookstores. Specifically, we will examine three such strategies: political framing, moral positioning, and cultural distinguishing. This chapter focuses on explaining the meaning, scope, and underlying rationale of these strategies, while a detailed analysis of their application by independent bookstores is presented in chapter 4. By employing these culturally adapted strategies, independent bookstores carve out a niche space in the highly competitive bookselling market, where their unique value propositions and offerings effectively differentiate them from other bookstores and afford them a crucial competitive advantage. These strategies thus have been critical to the rise and rapid development of independent bookstores over the last two decades.

POLITICAL FRAMING

The first major culturally adapted strategy that independent bookstores develop and deploy is *political framing*. It involves presenting their activities and offerings—such as the books they select and the events they organize—in explicit or implicit political terms. By infusing their stores with politically evocative elements and a notable sense of politicalness, they create an atmosphere that feels distinctly different and alternative. This atmosphere helps to differentiate independent bookstores from other kinds of bookstores and attracts customers who are drawn to such politically engaged and differentiated environments.

As discussed previously, the state's pronounced presence and influence are a key defining feature of China's cultural industry, including book publishing and bookselling. A range of rules and regulations are in place to govern activities in these sectors and ensure their lawful operations and orderly functioning to produce publicly beneficial cultural goods and services. In the book industry, guidelines, including *Chuban Guanli Tiaoli* (*Regulations on Publication Administration*) and *Chubanwu Shichang Guanli Guiding* (*Provisions on the Administration of the Publication Market*), regulate the activities of book publishers, distributors, wholesalers, and retailers alike by mandating licensing requirements, publication procedures, distribution and retailing protocols, and so forth. As a result, the measures affect the everyday practices of these players, shaping the range and variety of the end products and their dissemination on the market. Moreover, the involvement of state-owned players in this sector—most notably state-owned publishing houses and Xinhua Bookstores—shows the state's role in actively steering and shaping the development of China's book market by directly participating in the production and distribution of books and related services.

The state's presence and influence in the cultural industry, especially the private sector within it, have created tension with some practitioners who insist that cultural production should remain free from political influence. Some choose to resist this influence through confrontation and activism, criticizing and antagonizing state authority, sometimes in extreme and unlawful ways. Ironically, however, while these resisters advocate for a world where cultural production is "freed" from political influence, it is precisely this political influence they oppose that lends meaning and resonance to their activism. Others take a less radical stance. Rather than rejecting the state's presence in the cultural sphere altogether, they are more concerned about what they consider its homogenizing effect on cultural creation through its authority. These individuals tend to contend that the state's endeavor to provide guidelines for cultural production risks elevating a state-sanctioned mainstream culture above all other forms of culture, resulting in a homogeneous cultural milieu in China. As one independent bookshop owner said, "I don't believe that mainstream culture should be eliminated altogether. It has a right to exist, just like any other culture, view, and idea. The problem is that we don't have enough room for these alternative cultures, views, and ideas."

Several independent booksellers I interviewed shared this view. They had reservations about the political influence they observed in the Chinese book industry, considering it more or less constraining the industry's development. For example, more than one interviewee attributed the challenges faced by many physical bookstores in the digital age to the state's control over publishing. They contended that increased private-sector involvement in the publishing field could lead to a more diverse book market, which would allow physical, especially independent, bookstores greater choice in book selections, thereby enabling them to compete more effectively against online retailers.

While this argument may sound plausible, it is worth closer scrutiny. In particular, considering that China's publishing industry is already producing a colossal volume of books each year—204,667 new titles and 213,693 reprints in 2019—and that more than 45 percent of these titles sell fewer than ten copies annually, it is not convincing that a lack of diversity in publishing is the root cause of independent bookstores' difficulties in competing with online retailers.[1] Conversely, a more pressing issue here appears to be inefficiencies in the book supply chain. As I demonstrate in chapter 5, the core challenge facing many independent bookstores in China is not necessarily competition from state-owned or online bookstores but the absence of a book supply chain via which these small booksellers can stock books efficiently and cost-effectively. Compared to the alleged homogenization in publishing, supply-chain inefficiency has a more direct and detrimental effect on independent bookstores' abilities to compete and thrive.[2]

Despite their reservations about the state's influence in the book industry, few independent booksellers see it as their responsibility to challenge this power structure. As business owners, their priority is to keep their businesses afloat. To do so, they sometimes choose to maneuver certain political restrictions to please their customers (e.g., inviting politically controversial authors to events). Moreover, as privately owned enterprises, they can be automatically positioned as alternatives to state players, thereby acquiring a politicized image—whether by choice or not. These traits and endeavors of independent bookstores resonate with certain members of the public who patronize bookstores seeking not only reading materials but also spaces for social participation. To attract these customers, some independent bookstores deliberately downplay their economic attributes to emphasize their role as open forums for social, public, and even political engagement. Over time, underscoring this socio-political function has evolved into a business strategy adopted by more independent bookstores seeking to attract these socio-politically concerned customers, customers who both advertise for these stores' alternative offerings and contribute to their sales. Viewed from this perspective, what began as an effort by some independent bookstores to promote social and public participation has developed into a strategy of political framing that serves the economic goal of attracting and retaining customers—a goal that, for many adopters, is more relevant than the original vision.

The strategy of political framing can affect how independent bookstores select books, organize events, and design and decorate their stores. Bookshops adopting a political framing strategy often exude a distinct sense of politicalness, differentiating them from other bookstores. It is a choice rather than an inherent quality of or a prerequisite for these establishments. Owners or managers of independent bookstores can decide whether to adopt this strategy or not and how to implement it. For instance, while some bookstores might prominently display politically charged slogans to create a pronounced political atmosphere, others may only subtly hint at their stance by featuring politically controversial books in prime locations. By naming this strategy "political framing," I want to highlight its economic rationale and utility. The term *framing* implies that, unlike a political act, which is driven by explicit political motives, the strategy of political framing is primarily underlain by an economic objective: It enables independent bookstores to better compete by presenting themselves as socio-politically engaged to distinguish themselves from competitors. It serves as a marketing strategy, allowing these bookstores to attract target customers by casting themselves as unique and alternative players in the Chinese bookselling market.

That said, though not politically driven, political framing can produce socio-political effects. Most notably, it can transform independent bookstores into public spaces where members of the public can freely enter to engage with issues and ideas of broader social, public, or political relevance. Customers can do so by browsing the meticulously selected book collections, participating in carefully curated events, or gathering in the in-store cafés—facilities that are commonplace in independent bookstores—to engage in meaningful conversations. The specific nature of the issues and ideas explored—whether political or not—is secondary. From this standpoint, independent bookstores adopting the strategy of political framing can generate a political impact by facilitating the expression and circulation of ideas. Some independent bookstores make more efforts to generate more tangible socio-political effects. For example, more than one interviewee described to me how they would select and promote books that align with their political views as a means of expressing and influencing. Additionally, some bookstores host events for controversial authors, independent artists, or subculture practitioners, providing a platform for marginalized voices to be heard and debated. As a result, diverse and nonmainstream ideas and perspectives can often find a home in independent bookstores because of the strategy of political framing.

MORAL POSITIONING

The second major culturally adapted strategy that independent bookstores develop and deploy is moral positioning. It describes the processes in which independent bookstores give moral meanings to their activities and cast themselves as morally committed to differentiate themselves from other types of bookstores. To understand this strategy, we must unpack the meanings of the terms *moral* and *positioning* in this specific context.

Two Moral Visions

In the most common sense, the term *moral* can be synonymous with such terms as *good*, *right*, *virtuous*, *ethical*, or *appropriate*. Describing an individual as moral or as behaving morally generally suggests that they act according to widely accepted principles of rightness and goodness. This understanding is often commonly held within a community. Similarly, to moralize an object, action, or behavior is to regard it as morally righteous. In the context of independent bookselling in China, two moral visions emerge to be particularly relevant. First, independent bookstores perceive themselves as having an educational role to play in society. Second, viewing books as a special type of commodity that is imbued with their producers' intellectual, physical, and emotional labor, independent bookstores call for more respect for books and their creators and refuse to rely on aggressive price-cutting to compete.

THE EDUCATIONAL VISION

The educational vision held by many independent booksellers is best captured by their belief that, as book retailers, they serve as crucial cultural intermediaries in society who bear a responsibility to guide their customers to read intellectually beneficial books. Several interviewees compared this role with that of an educator, with one bookshop owner stating:

> We always say that teachers are the engineers of the human soul. I think that booksellers ought to play a similar role. Most people leave school at the age of eighteen or twenty-two. So who's going to be their teacher and help them learn and progress after that? I'd say that booksellers should aim to do that, and we're well-equipped to do so. By finding good books for our customers,

and by organizing events where readers can come together and exchange ideas, bookstores can and should be societal classrooms where citizens can come to learn and improve themselves.

Not everyone, however, identified equally with this educator role. When I paraphrased the above comment to other interviewees, most agreed that a bookseller has a duty to provide readers with intellectually uplifting books. Yet they found the idea that this role thus makes booksellers educators to be lofty and even arrogant. One interviewee remarked: "I wouldn't describe myself as anyone's teacher. I'm just a bookseller, and it is my job to select the best books and share them with my customers. But to say that I am therefore their teacher is an exaggeration and too lofty."

Like this interviewee, most independent bookstore owners or managers I spoke to defined their educational vision in terms of selecting and recommending worthy books rather than positioning themselves as quasi-educators. They carefully distinguish between exerting an educative influence by making high-quality books available and actively trying to educate and edify customers. A recurring theme in my interviews regarding the booksellers' motivations for entering bookselling was the gratification they derived from facilitating access to intellectually elevated reading materials rather than prescribing which books customers should read—as though they held some form of cultural authority.

That said, recommending which books are worth reading is not deemed a taboo by Chinese independent booksellers. This attitude contrasts sharply with that of their Western counterparts. According to Laura Miller, for modern-day independent booksellers in the United States, even suggesting to customers which books are worth reading is considered a condescending act and should be avoided at all costs.³ In China, however, this practice is fully appropriate and accepted by both independent booksellers and their patrons. In fact, many nonindependent booksellers I spoke with similarly noted that what differentiates bookselling from other businesses is its educative and moral impact on customers.

This widespread attitude has cultural roots. To begin with, books have been revered in China for more than three millennia; therefore, even the most profit-oriented booksellers would acknowledge the cultural significance of their trade and regard themselves as different from merchants dealing in other types of goods. The cultural significance attributed to the book business stems from a book's capacity to affect one's intellectual and spiritual well-being. Guiding customers toward reading edifying and uplifting texts is therefore considered an inherent and integral part of the bookselling profession. Beyond this cultural significance, bookselling also carries moral ramifications. This influence extends beyond the intellectual enrichment and augmentation that good books can bring to readers. It also concerns the harmful impact of bad books on readers. Consequently, a key responsibility of booksellers is to help readers differentiate between beneficial and detrimental reading materials. While the criteria for making such assessments can vary and even trigger debates, the underlying consensus remains that booksellers have a duty to guide their readers to read beneficial books for the betterment of both themselves and wider society.

Independent booksellers not only recognize the cultural and moral significance of their trade but also extend this understanding by linking it to another crucial function of books in traditional Chinese culture and society: promoting social advancement. Throughout China's more than five thousand years of history, books and book reading have been associated with having a successful and meaningful life. This was especially true for the learned men, known as *dushu ren* (people who read books), in that, by excelling at reading and writing, they could be selected by the emperor to serve as officials—a goal widely held as the highest form of achievement and ultimately the life goal of any learned man in ancient China. From the 580s to the early 1900s, the practice of book reading, or *dushu*—in the specific sense of studying the designated Confucian classics with the aim of succeeding in the imperial examinations to secure official roles—attained unparalleled social significance, for it served as the sole pathway for most educated men to ascend the social hierarchy and bring honor, wealth, and recognition to themselves, their families, and their ancestors. This sentiment is vividly expressed in a famous Chinese saying: "Within books, one can find tons of millet. Within books, one can find houses of gold. Within books, one can find admirers and servants. Within books, one can find ladies as fair as jade."[4] These words were composed by an emperor of the Song dynasty (960–1279) to motivate young men of the reading class to master the Confucian classics, succeed in the imperial exams, and obtain official appointments. They expressly convey how, through diligent study and reading, one can attain an ideal life marked by affluence, high social status, power, and a harmonious family life.

The Chinese's reverence for books and book reading, therefore, has deep cultural and historical roots. For this reason, it still resonates strongly in the present day. It is evident, for example, in Chinese people's widespread emphasis on academic study and success. However, unlike our ancestors, modern-day Chinese now embrace a more diversified notion of success. As a result, the social significance of books and book reading has broadened in scope. Rather than narrowly focusing on bringing worldly rewards, it now encompasses a wider range of meanings, including, for instance, enabling individuals to become better citizens capable of meaningful social and public participation through utilizing one's intellectual faculties to assimilate information, reason logically, and think critically. This broadened attitude informs many independent bookstores' vision to help readers develop these cognitive capabilities by providing beneficial reading materials. In the next chapter, we will return to this point when examining how moral positioning influences independent bookstores' book selection practices.

THE RESPECTFUL VISION

The social significance of books and book reading is pertinent to another distinctive, book-related culture in traditional Chinese society: reverence for writing and paper with written words on it. This tradition is most clearly embodied in the practice of *jingxi zizhi* (敬惜字纸), which literally means "respecting and cherishing written characters and paper." According to Alexander Des Forges, the practice of jingxi zizhi emerged around the Ming dynasty (1368–1644). Its core principle is that written words, and by extension, paper bearing them, should be treated with profound respect and never discarded as mere refuse, for doing so would taint the purity of the paper and the writing on it. Rather than throwing away unwanted paper with writing on it, people were expected to collect it carefully, burn it in a special furnace, and release the ashes into clean water bodies like rivers, lakes, or oceans to ensure that no impurity would defile the writing.[5]

Des Forges identified both cultural and religious underpinnings to this practice.[6] Religiously, it resonates with the Daoist ritual of burning paper inscribed with sacred texts. The cultural association, however, is more significant. As discussed above, mastery of the Confucian classics was essential for those seeking success in the imperial examinations in ancient China.

These exams required candidates to compose extensive handwritten essays, with only the highest-scoring participants having the prospect of ultimately securing official appointments. The competition was fierce: in the Qing dynasty (1644–1912), fewer than one in a thousand candidates who advanced through the local, provincial, and national examinations would eventually be appointed as officials.[7] Because the stakes were so high and so much hinged on one's written work, any practice believed to enhance one's fortunes in these exams was taken seriously. Thus, jingxi zizhi arose as a means of cultivating good luck and averting misfortune. Disrespecting written words or the paper bearing them was thought to bring bad luck in imperial examinations while showing reverence for them would conversely attract good luck.

The element of superstition in the emergence and spreading of the practice of jingxi zizhi is a topic for cultural historians and sinologists to explore. It might have played an important role in its spreading among the general populace. However, as Des Forges has found, the ritual of collecting and burning paper with written words was practiced not only by the educated class but also by those who were illiterate.[8] These individuals would never have the opportunity to participate in the imperial examinations, yet they embraced the practice nevertheless. From this viewpoint, we can argue that the tradition of jingxi zizhi reflected a general reverence in traditional Chinese culture for written words and for culture more broadly.

Viewed from a critical perspective, the veneration of written words—which were historically monopolized by the ruling class across cultures—can lend itself to a negative reading. It can be argued that this reverence, although seemingly benign, was effectively a form of deference manufactured and promoted by the dominated classes toward the domination, authority, and legitimacy of the ruling class. Lu Xun, one of China's most influential modern novelists and literary critics, for example, once criticized the practice of jingxi zizhi in an essay: "Written words belong to the privileged minority. They thus acquired a sense of dignity and mystery. The sense of the dignity of written words make those who can use them dignified and venerated."[9] This critique suggests that the practice not only instilled respect for writing and culture but also contributed to their mystification. As Vladimir Lenin pointed out in *The State and Revolution*, mystification is a potent tool used by the ruling class to normalize, justify, and preserve their domination.[10] Examined from this critical lens, conflicting cultural interpretations and characterizations of jingxi zizhi emerge as a valuable cultural tradition worthy of preservation, on the one hand and as a regressive cultural relic, on the other. This duality underscores the complex socio-cultural tapestry inherent in this specific tradition and in many other cultural practices and traditions.

The evaluation of jingxi zizhi aside, it is clear that while this tradition was once highly influential, its impact has largely faded in contemporary China. The special furnaces once used for burning paper now serve mainly as historical artifacts. Many younger people may have never heard of jingxi zizhi, let alone practiced it. For this reason, I was surprised when one of my interviewees cited this tradition as a reason why they believe books must be treated differently from other commodities and with more respect. This bookseller remarked: "We have the tradition of jingxi zizhi in China. It means that we must treat paper with written words on it with great respect. A book is essentially a collection of paper with writing on it, so we must respect it. You can't sell books the way you sell cabbages [to say something is like a cabbage in Chinese is to say it is very cheap and not valuable]. If you do, where is your respect for culture?"

Influenced by the jingxi zizhi tradition, this interviewee viewed books as a special kind of commodity that should not be valued solely by price. They continued: "The online bookstores often discount books by 50 percent, 60 percent, 70 percent, or even 80 percent. Some discount bookstores sell books at a fixed price, like 5 yuan per title. Others even sell books by weight, like 5 yuan per kilogram. This is ridiculous. This is outrageous. We're talking about books, not cabbages. No one should be allowed to sell books by weight!"

Of course, one doesn't need to adhere to jingxi zizhi to see that books are a special kind of commodity deserving greater respect and care and to sympathize with this frustrated bookseller. Several customers I spoke with too considered it inappropriate to sell books at prices drastically below not only their listed prices but also their value as defined by the labor that went into their creation. A shared sentiment was that, as a cultural commodity, books differ from other types of goods because of the extensive efforts invested in their production. Respecting books, therefore, is to respect the mental, intellectual, and oftentimes emotional labor that authors, editors, and others put into the creation of a book. While physical labor matters as well, it is primarily the intellectual and emotional labor invested that makes books unique: Beyond their economic value, books embody human intellect, imagination, and creativity. In this light, it is easy to understand why so many independent booksellers I interviewed emphasized that they did more than just sell books—they also respected them—and an important way of showing their respect was by refusing to sell books at steep discounts. They contend that by refusing to undersell to compete, they show their respect toward both the books and their creators. The second moral vision held by China's independent bookstores, therefore, is a vision of respect, a vision that is fundamentally rooted in their esteem for culture and creativity.

Another cause of this vision concerns unfair competition. Several independent booksellers I interviewed argued that aggressive discounting by online retailers is unethical because it distorts the market and undermines the entire publishing ecosystem. Unlike professional bookstores, which depend on book sales for profit, large online retailers often use books as loss leaders to entice customers to their sites to purchase other higher-margin products. This is considered unethical because while these platforms can easily offset their book-related losses with other sales, most professional bookstores lack the financial means and stability to weather their aggressive competition. In other words, the playing field is unlevel. One interviewee explained this with an analogy: "We're forced to compete in a race that cannot be won. It's like racing an old bicycle against a Ferrari. We stand no chance of winning, for we're not competing against another old bicycle—we are up against an automobile. This kind of competition would never happen in real sports, but it's happening in book retailing." Some independent booksellers, therefore, considered their refusal to join the price war a principled, even noble, act. They hope their determination can help preserve the integrity of an industry they care about and demonstrate to publishers, authors, and readers alike the possibility of restoring the disrupted order in the book market. Admittedly, for most of these bookstores, their decision to abstain from steep discounts is underlain by an economic reality: They simply cannot afford to sell books at very low prices. Even so, their refusal to add more fuel to the price war deserves recognition, and underlying their determination is a shared belief in the moral duties of book retailers.

Positioning

Having analyzed the meaning of *moral* in the strategy of moral positioning, let's conclude this section by exploring the meaning of *positioning*. In this context, positioning signifies that independent bookstores, by interpreting their roles in distinctive moral terms, strive to distinguish themselves from other types of bookstores. That is, the process of moralization helps to contrast and differentiate independent bookstores from their competitors. Specifically, the educational vision helps to distinguish independent bookstores from the profit-oriented bookstores that sell books solely for financial gains, while the respectful vision contrasts independent bookstores with the discounters, especially the large online bookselling platforms. From this perspective, although many independent booksellers consider these two moral visions as inherent to the independent identity, the process of moralization and the strategy of moral positioning serve a significant economic purpose: enabling independent bookstores to better compete by highlighting their unique and alternative offerings, ones with a distinctive moral dimension.

CULTURAL DISTINGUISHING

The third and final culturally adapted strategy that independent bookstores develop and deploy is cultural distinguishing. It describes how these bookstores construct their offerings—books, other goods, services, and store aesthetics—to appeal to customers seeking a sense of cultural distinction through consumption. Like political framing and moral positioning, cultural distinguishing enables independent bookstores to better compete by accentuating their unique attributes and differences from their competitors, especially the nonindependent bookstores.

As I will demonstrate in chapter 4, independent bookstores employ cultural distinguishing to mark their difference from their competitors in several dimensions. First, they prioritize quality over profit when selecting books. Compared with nonindependent bookstores and online retailers, independent bookstores are celebrated for their high-quality book collections. This appeals to customers seeking not only great books but also enriching cultural experiences through book shopping. Second, independent bookstores provide customers with enriching cultural experiences by hosting diverse cultural events. Apart from standard bookstore events like author tours, independent bookstores routinely host a variety of events and activities—ranging from poetry readings to tea tastings, yoga classes, exhibitions, concerts, and live performances—to transform themselves into multifunctional cultural hubs and capitalize on the growing market for experience-based cultural consumption. Finally, the enriching cultural experience offered by independent bookstores is often enhanced by these stores' aesthetic interior design and attractive environments. Elements such as soothing music, pleasant scents, warm lighting, and comfortable seating make these bookstores appealing to consumers seeking not just quality reading material but also a unique shopping experience. Many independent bookstores have become popular social media photo spots for their stylish interiors. The cultural distinction of independent bookstores can also extend beyond mere aesthetics. Some independents, for example, are remembered by the rich cultural meanings and messages they embed in their store designs, effectively turning space-making into a process of meaning-making and expression.

Next, I draw upon the theoretical frameworks of Pierre Bourdieu and Thorstein Veblen to analyze the social and economic drivers behind the development of the strategy of cultural distinguishing.

Two Sets of Logic

Cultural institutions like museums, theatres, galleries, and bookstores serve as venues where individuals engage in cultural experiences by acquiring and consuming cultural goods and services. Due to the dual nature of cultural goods as both commodities and forms of artistic expression, these cultural institutions operate under two interlinked and yet distinct logics: economic logic and cultural logic.

Governed by economic logic, cultural institutions operate much like businesses. They offer products or services to deliver value to customers in exchange for profit. Even not-for-profit cultural institutions financed by charities or government bodies must adopt viable business models to generate the revenue needed to sustain their daily operations. The profits yielded by the sale of goods and services hence constitute a main source of these cultural institutions' economic capital. Drawing on Bourdieu's definition, economic capital refers to an individual's or an organization's financial and material resources, such as money, real estate, and shares and stocks.[11] Cultural institutions may also derive economic capital from other avenues, such as donations, subsidies, investments, and crowdfunding. Regardless of its source, economic capital is as vital to cultural institutions as it is to any other enterprise, for they need it to remain financially and operationally viable.

Governed by cultural logic, a primary goal of cultural institutions is to produce cultural artifacts and practices to create and deliver cultural and artistic value to their audiences. This logic prioritizes cultural and artistic merit over economic return and is characterized by Bourdieu as the "autonomous principle" of cultural production.[12] Operating under this principle, cultural institutions with higher levels of cultural and artistic excellence tend to enjoy greater recognition and prestige—from both their peers and the public—than those emphasizing economic rewards and consequently garnering little external recognition. The recognition and prestige conferred upon cultural institutions constitute their symbolic capital. This capital is crucial in that it reflects and signals a cultural institution's cultural and artistic competence and thereby establishes its standing relative to other cultural institutions, including competitors, within the hierarchy of cultural excellence. In this hierarchy, those organizations with greater symbolic capital occupy higher positions and can exert greater influence in shaping the rules and standards for evaluating cultural and artistic merit. This invaluable cultural authority, unattainable by economic means, underscores the unparalleled significance of symbolic capital to cultural institutions.

Most cultural institutions operate under both economic and cultural logic and endeavor to accumulate both forms of capital. However, how these logics affect a particular cultural institution and influence its pursuit of economic vis-à-vis symbolic capital can vary significantly. Generally speaking, cultural institutions oriented toward profit-making are more strongly guided by economic logic, which enables them to garner more economic capital than cultural recognition and prestige. In contrast, cultural institutions guided by a commitment to artistic excellence are more deeply influenced by cultural logic, which affords them greater symbolic capital but reduced financial means and stability. Independent bookstores tend to exemplify the latter type of cultural institutions in that, by contrast with nonindependent bookstores and online retailers, they typically hold higher levels of symbolic capital while persistently struggling to make a profit. This uneven distribution of economic and symbolic capital is a key feature of these bookstores and profoundly shapes their behavior, including the development and deployment of the strategy of cultural distinguishing.

Economic and Cultural Capital of the Independent Bookstore

Compared to other types of bookstores in the Chinese bookselling field—primarily Xinhua Bookstores, nonindependent privately owned bookstores, and online retailers—independent bookstores as a whole generally hold the lowest levels of economic capital. Several factors contribute to this situation. First, bookselling in China typically has low profit margins. For example, selling books acquired at a 35 percent stocking discount at full price yields a gross profit margin of 35 percent. However, since most independent bookstores receive smaller discounts from their suppliers—usually between 25 percent and 30 percent—and often sell books at a further discount to customers (around 5–10 percent), their gross profit margins tend to fall below 25 percent, usually around 20 percent.

This low gross profit margin, combined with the relatively low price of books in China, underlies the low profitability of most independent bookstores. In 2019, the median book price in China was 45 yuan (approximately US$7.07).[13] Even at a 35 percent margin, the gross profit from selling books at full price remains modest. For instance, selling a 40-yuan book acquired at a 35 percent discount would yield a mere gross profit of 14 yuan (approximately US$2) without a discount to customers or 10 yuan if a 10 percent discount is applied. With such narrow margins, bookstores need high sales volumes to turn a profit.

To achieve high sales volumes, most nonindependent bookstores prioritize study aid books, children's books, or other bestselling genres—these are the types of books that can usually deliver high sales. Xinhua Bookstores and large online retailers also benefit from extra advantages, such as better discount terms, larger sales, and additional revenue streams. None of these benefits, however, are available to independent bookstores, resulting in their constant struggle to generate sufficient revenues and profit. While it may be their choice not to sell the bestselling genres, several independent booksellers I interviewed expressed that access to other favorable terms, such as larger stocking discounts, would have been desired.

In contrast to their low economic capital, most independent bookstores possess rich symbolic capital. This is evidenced by their widespread reputation among readers, publishers, authors, and so on as purveyors of high-quality books. For readers, independent bookstores represent reliable sources for discovering great books, while authors and publishers, particularly those focused on serious nonfiction and literature, highly value when their works are stocked and recommended by independent bookstores, especially the renowned ones.

Independent bookstores garner symbolic capital not only through the books they commit to selling but also by forgoing those books they consider beneath their cultural standards. For example, literature, poetry, and serious nonfiction are prioritized in independent bookstores for their perceived higher cultural and intellectual value, even though they tend to generate modest sales. Meanwhile, independent bookstores collectively eschew the bestselling genres, seeing their market popularity as a sign of low cultural merit. In particular, they avoid study aid books, regarding them as devoid of "any intrinsic cultural and intellectual value," as radically put by one bookseller I interviewed. "I don't sell study aid books because they have no cultural value. They exist only to meet market demand and have no real value beyond that." From these perspectives, independent bookstores bolster their holdings of symbolic capital by distancing themselves from market demands and profit-driven motives. Although they recognize profit as a necessity for survival, they do not view it as their primary reason for operating. Their privileging of cultural value over profit and reluctance to maximize economic returns at the expense of their cultural pride, therefore, confer them substantial symbolic capital.

To sum up, independent bookstores are characterized by an uneven distribution of economic capital and symbolic capital, the two most important resources that shape the behavior of cultural institutions. As my analysis shows, these two forms of capital are closely intertwined: A reluctance to maximize profit (economic capital) facilitates the accumulation of symbolic capital. According to Bourdieu, different types of capital are mutually convertible under certain circumstances. I argue that the strategy of cultural distinguishing serves the purpose of converting symbolic capital to economic capital for independent bookstores by enabling them to attract customers who seek cultural distinction through the consumption of premium cultural good and services.

Distinction Through Consumption: Serving Culturally Discerned Customers

The social analysis of the relationship between consumption and socio-economic stratification is profoundly influenced by two theoretical approaches: Pierre Bourdieu's theory of distinction and Thorstein Veblen's theory of conspicuous consumption. Both theorists highlight the role of consumption in signaling social status and, therefore, establish a relationship between consumption practices and the production and reproduction of social inequalities. A major difference between these two approaches lies in their differing perspectives on the nature of consumption. While Veblen considers consumption a deliberate act individuals perform to display their economic affluence, social status, and symbolic prestige, Bourdieu sees consumption choices as structurally determined by one's objective socio-economic conditions. For him, consumption practices are largely predetermined and have "nothing to do with rational choice."[14] Compared with Bourdieu's theory, Veblen's approach seems to offer greater conceptual flexibility for analyzing the social roots of consumption.

CONSUMPTION AS A SOCIAL PRACTICE

At the core of Bourdieu's theory of distinction lies the idea that the hierarchy of tastes in cultural consumption (e.g., music, art, books, furniture) is rooted in the hierarchy of social and economic power held by different social classes. The upper, or dominant, class, possessing greater economic resources, is free from material constraints and hence can pursue cultural objects and practices that prioritize aesthetics over utility. Through their social authority, they establish their tastes as the most legitimate, a legitimacy ultimately grounded in their economic privilege rather than any inherent cultural value of the tastes per se. The dominant class's cultural tastes thus serve as tools of exclusion, preventing lower classes from partaking in similar cultural experiences and thereby reinforcing the cultural, social, and economic privileges and authority of the dominant class.

By contrast, the dominated class, constrained by their limited economic resources, must prioritize functionality over aesthetics in their cultural consumption. Their tastes are subsequently stigmatized as "low" by the upper class, which then serves to neutralize and perpetuate the cultural and economic disadvantages of the dominated class. For Bourdieu, this devaluation of lower-class cultural practices plays a key role in preserving the upper class's economic and social dominance.

The middle class often exhibits a degree of pretension in their tastes. They aspire to mimic the style of the upper class but typically lack sufficient economic and cultural capital to fully and authentically engage in the cultural practices sanctioned by the upper class. As a result, middle-class tastes are labeled "middle-brow," suggesting that they are neither fully lower-class nor entirely aligned with upper-class standards.

In Bourdieu's eyes, cultural preferences are not merely personal choices but are fundamentally embedded in unequal power relations. Cultural practices are hence shaped by one's class position and can only be fully understood through the lens of class stratification and struggle. Although Veblen also recognizes the role of class in shaping consumption behavior, he offers a more flexible framework for analyzing the social shaping of taste and consumption. Specifically, he introduces the concept of conspicuous consumption to explain how individuals squander—that is, purchase goods and services that exceed practical needs—to display or attain social status.[15] Conspicuous consumption, therefore, serves social goals rather than merely fulfilling immediate needs (e.g., buying food for sustenance), and it affects all social classes: both those that are already economically privileged and need to maintain their status and those seeking to ascend the social ladder through squandering. For the privileged class, conspicuous consumption not only flaunts their wealth but also signals their elevated social position conferred by that wealth—it serves to distinguish them from other classes. Meanwhile, for those seeking upward social mobility, conspicuous consumption allows them to gain entry into the higher echelon by mimicking the tastes of the higher class to gain recognition and acceptance.

In contrast to Bourdieu's view—where consumption is seen as heavily structured by class conditions and perpetuating existing social inequalities—Veblen's concept of conspicuous consumption acknowledges the role of agency and active choice in consumption behavior. His framework thus offers a more balanced account of the relationship between class and consumption. That is, while consumption choices remain deeply influenced by class positions, they are not entirely prescribed by them. Instead, consumers can exercise autonomy to express personal preferences and pursue social objectives that transcend their class positions. This framework thus enables us to analyze consumption as a dynamic sphere of action in which individuals actively navigate and negotiate the hierarchies of class and taste.

CONSPICUOUS CONSUMPTION AND PATRONIZING THE INDEPENDENT BOOKSTORE

Although the concept of conspicuous consumption—originally developed in the late nineteenth century to explain the spending behavior of the wealthy classes in industrial America—has drawn much criticism from contemporary sociologists and cultural economists, it remains a useful theoretical tool for considering how social factors shape consumption in the present day. In particular, it reveals the socio-economic logic behind what initially appears to be irrational spending. For Veblen, an "element of waste" is central to conspicuous consumption, for it showcases the spender's abundant economic, social, and cultural resources.[16] This way, conspicuous—or irrational—consumption ultimately serves to *impress* others: The affluent squander to display their status both among their peers and to those beneath them, while those seeking upward social mobility do so to gain recognition and acceptance. Ultimately, this desire to impress, which is rooted in a pursuit of social distinction, underlies not only conspicuous consumption but any consumption practice marked by an element of waste or economic inefficiency.

In the digital age, shopping in physical bookstores can be considered economically insufficient, for compared to the convenience of online shopping, purchasing books from brick-and-mortar bookstores often entails higher cost, more time, and greater effort, amounting to reduced economic efficiency. Similarly, reading physical books can be less efficient than reading e-books, owing to higher expenses, limited portability, and the extra effort of storage. To stretch this line of argument even further, one could contend that reading books—whether for information or entertainment—is less efficient than online searches or the vast digital media options widely available today.

Building on this line of logic, shopping for books at independent bookstores can be viewed as an act of conspicuous consumption, for customers here exhibit three defining features of conspicuous consumers: They disregard economic efficiency, seek a unique and distinguished cultural experience, and possess the necessary wealth, time, and cultural discernment to engage in and appreciate that experience. For these patrons, price is secondary. Their willingness to purchase items—books or other goods—at higher prices from independent bookstores showcases their choice to prioritize experiential value over economic efficiency. What they value more is the distinguished and distinguishing experience of discovering great books and other goods in a tastefully designed bookstore manned by courteous staff and frequented by individuals who share similar cultural tastes and socio-economic standing. These customers derive fulfillment and satisfaction that transcend the utilitarian appeal of online shopping. From this perspective, patronizing independent bookstores amounts to a form of conspicuous consumption where customers seek to impress and distinguish through their shopping practices.

If consumers visit independent bookstores to impress others and assert distinction, what kind of distinction do they seek? Drawing on Bourdieu, we can argue that this is a class-based form of distinction: Well-educated individuals from the upper and middle classes frequent independent bookstores as a way of signaling their refined cultural tastes. Indeed, Western observers of Chinese culture and economy have long linked the rise of the so-called middle-class consumer in China to various market phenomena and business trends, from the booming luxury market to a rapidly expanding coffee market.[17] Could the rise and development of independent bookstores also be explained by the middle-class consumer theory? In my view, while many customers of independent bookstores are indeed affluent and well-educated, their decision to frequent these establishments should not be reduced to a class-based choice.

First, the class-based explanation is not supported by my empirical data. From my interviews and observations, there is no strong evidence suggesting a class convergence among independent bookstore patrons. Although items sold in independent bookshops can be pricey, this does not in itself prove that their customers, on average, have higher economic status. Unlike luxury goods, which clearly signal affluence, the relatively higher prices of books and other goods typically sold in independent bookstores (e.g., designer stationery) remain affordable to a wide range of consumers. As one manager of an independent bookstore noted: "Our customer base is really diverse. There is a misperception that independent bookstores are for those stylish white-collar workers and middle-class consumers. In reality, many of our regular customers are university or high school students, stay-at-home mums, and retirees. I guess they have more free time than white-collar workers. So we try our best to serve readers from all walks of life, not just the middle class." The diverse composition of independent bookstore patrons suggests that these bookstores attract a variety of customers beyond just affluent, middle-class consumers. Patronizing independent bookstores, therefore, should not necessarily be associated with membership in a certain social class.

Second, the concept of middle-class consumers in China is imprecisely defined and inconsistently applied, limiting its explanatory power.[18] For example, a 2013 McKinsey report defines "middle-class consumers" in China as those earning an annual household disposable income of US$9,000 to US$34,000—a criterion expected to encompass 75 percent of all urban residents by 2022.[19] More recently, the *Hurun 2018 China New Middle-Class Report* states that an annual household income of more than RMB 300,000 (approximately US$41,820) is required to lead a middle-class lifestyle in Beijing, Shanghai, Shenzhen and Guangzhou, while an income of over RMB 200,000 (approximately US$27,880) is needed for residents of other large cities such as Chengdu, Hangzhou, Chongqing, Wuhan, Xi'an, Suzhou, and Tianjin.[20] While this income-based approach may be convenient for big-picture-style business projections, it is overly simplistic and too broad for analyzing nuanced consumer behaviors. Meanwhile, in academic literature, additional dimensions—such as geographic location, education, age, and occupation—have been incorporated to portray a more nuanced picture of China's middle class.[21] Yet these criteria can be too complicated and unwieldy for analyzing specific business phenomena. As a result, the concept of "middle-class consumer" does not lend itself as a robust framework for analyzing and understanding the development and practices of independent bookstores.

Instead of a class-based explanation, I consider that patrons of independent bookstores are motivated by a pursuit of cultural sophistication and individuality. Despite varying in class, income, education, occupation, and age, these customers share a common desire for unique and distinguishing cultural experiences. It is this shared desire for cultural distinction that drives them to patronize independent bookstores, while this sentiment, in turn, propels independent bookstores to tailor their offerings to better meet these customer needs—most notably by using the strategy of cultural distinguishing.

4

IMPLEMENTING CULTURALLY ADAPTED STRATEGIES

This chapter examines how independent bookstores implement the three culturally adapted strategies discussed in the last chapter in their daily business operations. Specifically, it demonstrates how these strategies affect the way they select books, host events, and design stores. I argue that aligning these activities with the principles of political framing, moral positioning, and cultural distinguishing enables independent bookstores to deliver some unique values for customers and, therefore, develop a crucial competitive advantage in the highly competitive bookselling market. From this perspective, although many of the practices examined below may appear to be driven by distinctive cultural visions, they fulfill critical economic purposes. This chapter highlights the importance of analyzing the mutual embeddedness of cultural and economic incentives via the concept of culturally adapted strategy for understanding the behavior of cultural enterprises like independent bookstores from a sociological lens.

BOOK CURATION

Curating, Not Just Stocking, Books

Selecting which books to stock is arguably the single most important decision a bookstore has to make on a daily basis. Few other retailers enjoy the same luxury as book retailers when it comes to choosing inventory from such an extensive selection of available products. In 2019, for example, a total of 505,979 books were published in China.[1] To put this into perspective, the largest single-store independent bookshop I visited housed approximately seventy thousand titles, including both titles displayed in-store and ones in a warehouse. In contrast, most small- and medium-sized independent bookstores I studied typically carried only a few thousand titles. Considering this stark disparity between the vast quantity of available books and the practical limits of titles a bookstore can reasonably carry, it is a question of whether the task of selecting several thousand titles from hundreds of thousands of options is a luxury or a challenge.

Regardless, effective book selection is undeniably a cornerstone of any bookstore, and performing it well is paramount. But what does it mean to select books "effectively," and why is it so important? Effective book selection entails two core elements and is vital for two reasons. First, it entails curating an inventory that will sell well so that the bookstore can make sufficient profit to achieve financial viability. Doing so requires a good grasp of customer needs and market trends, for bookstores want to select books with strong marketability and sales potential. This process is no different from how, for example, a car dealer selects vehicle models or a supermarket chooses which groceries to stock: They all base their decisions on an assessment of the potential products' marketability and profitability. The first core element of effective book selection, therefore, is a bookstore's ability to identify and select profitable books, and it serves a crucial economic function. Unlike car dealers or supermarkets, however, bookstores are not merely economic entities. Many are also committed to delivering noneconomic values—cultural, artistic, political, ethical, or religious—that extend beyond profitability. Effective book selection, therefore, also entails curating an inventory that aligns with and promotes these broader values. This cultural dimension of book selection reflects the unique role bookstores play in society in fostering cultural and intellectual engagement, making the second function of effective book selection culturally bound.

This dimension highlights a key difference between bookstores and most other types of retailers: Whereas other retailers typically prioritize economic returns in their inventory selection, bookstores often seek both economic and cultural values in their offerings. For instance, while a car dealer promoting electric vehicles or a supermarket specializing in organic foods may do so because they value sustainability or ethical practices, such decisions are often driven primarily by profitability rather than purely noneconomic motives. That is, it is the higher profitability of the relevant goods instead of ethical considerations that underpins these choices. In contrast, bookstores frequently place equal or greater emphasis on their cultural considerations. While economic considerations remain crucial, the integration of noneconomic values into their business decisions distinguishes bookstores as both cultural and commercial enterprises guided by a dual approach to value creation.

These principles are particularly manifest in independent bookstores. Many of the independent bookstores I studied routinely stocked books they knew would sell modestly but still stocked them for their cultural values instead of economic ones.

Although, as I will discuss in chapter 5, economic considerations are crucial for these bookstores, they often have less impact on book selection compared to other aspects of their operations. In fact, book selection is the one domain where economic considerations yield to the pursuit of noneconomic values and objectives. Therefore, for independent bookstores, effective book selection means choosing titles that contribute to their cultural commitment, even when such choices often result in economic loss.

Some might interpret this practice as altruistic: bookstores sacrificing profit to promote lesser-known but worthy books. However, the independent booksellers I interviewed offered a more nuanced perspective. They emphasized that their decisions were not altruistic but grounded in sound business reasoning. Making less popular but worthy books available aligns with their core motive for entering the bookselling business, which is not to amass wealth but to find fulfillment in connecting readers with valuable books, especially ones unavailable at large commercial or online bookstores. This fulfillment is not entirely altruistic, for it gives these booksellers a deep sense of pride and purpose. Moreover, for many independent booksellers, bookselling is not a mere commercial activity but also a cultural and creative endeavor—a way to cultivate culture, explore ideas, and exercise creativity. Carefully curating an inventory thus serves as their way of engaging in the broader culture-making process. This, too, is not purely altruistic, as it allows these individuals to realize their personal passions while creating value for others. Finally, as I have iterated previously, independent bookstores' book selections serve an important economic purpose of attracting distinction-seeking customers. Once in the store, these generous customers often purchase the more profitable nonbook merchandise sold alongside the books. In this way, these books act as catalysts for generating additional revenue streams and supporting the overall viability of the bookstores.

From this perspective, book selection by independent bookstores carries both economic and cultural significance, benefiting not just the bookstores but also the communities they serve, including readers, authors, and suppliers. Book selection thus transcends mere inventory management; it is a creative process of curation and reimagination. Independent bookstores assess, select, and organize books in ways that infuse them with new meanings and values. Hence, while authors create the books, the curated inventory is the creative work of the bookstore, which reinterprets and reshapes existing materials. This creativity also extends to how books are physically arranged and displayed in the bookstores. Like artistic curation, the act of assembling and showcasing books becomes as important as the books themselves in transmitting meanings and ideas. Independent bookstores, through curation, transform inventory selection into a form of cultural and creative expression that enriches their communities and redefines the role of retail in cultural life.

John Thompson once discussed the impact of book placement on sales. He found out that prime locations, such as front-of-store tables, stepladders, and central display areas, can greatly boost a title's visibility and sales. Recognizing this, publishers are willing to pay substantial premiums to secure these coveted spots for their books, hoping this will drive sales. For example, according to Thompson, a prominent position on a front-of-store table across all branches of a major US chain bookstore can cost a publisher approximately $10,000 for a two-week period. Less central locations, while still valuable, cost around $3,500. These prices can escalate further for highly sought-after spots like a stepladder display, which can command as much as $25,000 for just one week.[2]

This practice of selling prime display space for enhanced visibility is common in many retail businesses but remains relatively uncommon in the bookselling industry in China. Some large Xinhua Bookstore branches may require higher discounts from publishers for placing their books on front-of-store tables, but such practices are far from widespread across the sector. None of the independent bookstores I studied engaged in this practice, and most interviewees were not even aware of its existence. In most independent bookstores, display decisions are entirely internal, guided by a mix of cultural and economic considerations. Economically, prime locations are typically reserved for newly arrived books to capture customers' attention and signal that the store offers fresh stock. Emphasizing the importance of regularly refreshing front-of-store displays, one interviewee described to me how they sometimes simply rotated older stock to create a sense of novelty for customers. Additionally, popular titles expected to generate large sales naturally occupy prominent spots. Culturally, book placement can hold deeper significance. As I will explore further, many independent bookstores use displays to express ideas, make statements, or showcase their creativity, turning book arrangement into a form of cultural expression.

Prioritizing Scholarly Books: An Act of Moral Positioning and Political Framing

According to Laura Miller, when it comes to book selection, US booksellers consider a variety of factors, including price, discounts, authors' sales history, popularity of similar genres or topics, payment and returns terms, publishers' marketing plans, and various indicators of books' quality. Of all the factors influencing booksellers' stocking decisions, Miller notes, "only some are related to the book's content."³ This observation highlights a common practice in bookselling: Most booksellers evaluate books primarily as commodities and base their stocking decisions on the expected commercial performance of candidate titles. While independent bookstores are known for valuing the book's editorial quality more than their commercially driven counterparts, as Miller finds, even the independents strive to balance between cultural quality and sales potential.

This economic mode of book selection is universal and can be observed in many nonindependent bookstores in China as well. For example, when asked about their book selection criteria, a buyer at a privately owned bookstore chain stated: "When you have eighteen stores to stock for, all you can and should consider is which books will sell and sell fast, and these are the books you want to stock. You don't have time to judge every title's content to decide if it's good or not. For me, good books are books that sell a lot of copies." This response highlights how commercially driven bookstores typically prioritize sales potential over editorial merit, assessing books primarily as goods for profit generation.

In contrast, independent bookstores adopt a markedly different approach, viewing books not merely as commodities but as cultural and intellectual artifacts. For them, content is the chief determinator in their selection process, while factors like sales potential, price, and discounts play only a secondary role. As such, when asked about their selection criteria, many independent booksellers I interviewed simply said that they chose "good books." But what do they mean by that? While this term is subjective and open to various interpretations, a consensus did emerge: That is, when it comes to book selection, China's independent bookstores prioritize what they call "scholarly books."

DEFINING "SCHOLARLY BOOKS"

The independent bookstores I studied demonstrated a strong preference for scholarly books. Over two-thirds of the bookstore owners or managers I interviewed identified that these books constituted the majority of their inventory and were prioritized over other types of books in book selection. "*Xueshu shu* [scholarly books] is our top priority. They make up 70 percent to 80 percent of our book collection. The remaining 20 percent consists of literature, poetry, and good quality bestsellers," said the owner of a small independent bookshop in Suzhou, a city near Shanghai. For some, scholarly books were so important that they considered it a defining feature of independent bookstores.

Despite this wide consensus on the significance of scholarly books for independent bookstores, a precise and clear-cut definition of this term is lacking. Most independent booksellers use it broadly to refer to books with distinctive intellectual content, including both academic monographs and serious nonfiction. *Xueshu shu*, therefore, are not the same as academic books as typically defined in the English-language book publishing industry, which refers to academic monographs or long-form academic texts written by and for academics for research purposes.[4] For China's independent booksellers, *xueshu shu* include both academic texts written by and for academics and books aimed at a broader readership but with scholarly or intellectual depth, similar to serious nonfiction in the English-language book publishing context.

This unique scope of scholarly books arises from the blurred boundaries in the Chinese book publishing industry between academic monographs, on the one hand, and general interest books with in-depth intellectual content, on the other. As discussed in chapter 1, books published in China are classified into eight broad categories: social science, science and technology, literature and art, Chinese classics, children's books, education, academic, and reference/encyclopedias. Except for children's books, each of the other seven categories includes both general-interest books (trade books in English-language publishing) and books for professional or specialized audiences. Publishers specializing in one category can produce both formats of books. For example, a publisher specializing in astronautics can publish both academic monographs and popular science books in the field of astronautics, and all these books are classified as science and technology books and distributed through the same channels. In terms of academic books as defined in English-language publishing—such as the Chinese translations of Max Weber's *The Protestant Ethic and the Spirit of Capitalism* and Michel Foucault's *Discipline and Punish*—they are often classified as both academic and social science books if their content aligns with the social science disciplines. So while these texts are academic in nature, they may be sold alongside mass-market social science titles like self-help guides. These examples show that in the Chinese book publishing industry, the categorization of books is based predominantly on content rather than format. As such, *xueshu shu* tends to encompass both academic books (academic texts written by and for academics) and general-interest books with in-depth intellectual content (serious nonfiction). I use the term "scholarly books" to refer to *xueshu shu* to distinguish it from "academic books" as typically understood in the English-language publishing context.

Some independent booksellers associate scholarly books with humanities and social sciences disciplines specifically, especially philosophy, history, law, economics, sociology, media studies, political science, anthropology, and so on, as opposed to science, technology, engineering, and mathematics (STEM) disciplines. Alternatively, some booksellers use the term more broadly to include any serious works that address issues of social, public, or political relevance. Under this expanded use, even serious literature may qualify as scholarly books. For instance, one interviewee described George Orwell's political novels *1984* and *Animal Farm* as examples of scholarly books.

With a clearer understanding of the meaning of scholarly books, our next question is: Why do independent bookstores emphasize these books, and what role do they play in these establishments?

First, some booksellers noted that scholarly books can be profitable. This is partly because publishers typically offer lower discounts on these books compared to the steep discounts given to other categories, such as study aid books, children's books, and general bestsellers. As a result, even online bookstores rarely sell these books at high discounts, resulting in relative price consistency across different retail channels. This consistency allows physical bookstores, especially independents, to remain price-competitive in this niche market. Additionally, the typical readers of scholarly books often possess higher levels of education and greater financial resources, making them relatively less sensitive to price differences and more likely to become loyal patrons of bookstores that provide high-quality book selections. As one bookstore manager in Beijing observed: "These customers aren't overly concerned about prices. If they find a book they like, they'll just buy it from us rather than ordering online to save a few yuan. This helps with our sales."

However, not everyone shared this perspective. Some argued that the modest sales of scholarly books often failed to offset the benefits of their higher per-copy profit margins. Furthermore, the impact of these books on attracting affluent customers was seen as inconsistent and difficult to measure. As one interviewee remarked: "If I wanted to make more profits, I'd just sell study aid books or children's books—these are the real profit generators. You'll never make a lot of money from selling xueshu shu because they never sell in large volumes." Notably, this interviewee's bookstore lacked a large inventory of nonbook merchandise and an in-store café. Such nonbook products and services, however, are often essential for fully maximizing the value of scholarly books, for they help convert customer traffic into more sales.

While some independent bookstores derive tangible economic benefits from scholarly books, economic considerations are rarely their primary motivation for stocking these titles. Instead, their emphasis on these books is primarily driven by a desire to establish distinctive identities and differentiate themselves from their competitors and is closely linked to the culturally adapted strategies of moral positioning and political framing.

SCHOLARLY BOOKS AND MORAL POSITIONING

As discussed in the last chapter, the strategy of moral positioning comprises two core dimensions, or visions: the educational vision and the respectful vision. The educational vision describes independent booksellers' commitment to providing intellectually uplifting reading materials to benefit customers. Scholarly books thus align with this vision in that their intellectual content serves to nourish their readers' minds rather than providing mere entertainment. The respectful vision, on the other hand, characterizes independent booksellers' rejection of commercialism in bookselling. It involves practices such as prioritizing cultural value over profit and avoiding heavy discounts. Scholarly books thus align with this vision not only because they are the epitome of high-quality publications privileging cultural standards over market appeal but also because bookstores stocking them often do so with a conscious acknowledgment of their modest sales potential.

Moreover, by stocking scholarly books, independent bookstores actively intervene in what they perceive as an overly commercial order in the Chinese bookselling market. By providing critical retail space to these culturally worthy but often unprofitable books, they also support the authors and publishers who produce these works. This sentiment was captured by one bookseller from Qingdao, Shandong Province, who remarked: "To be honest with you, I want to make money and be rich, too. Who doesn't? But once you're in the business and see that most bookstores sell only those study aid books and bestsellers, you begin to feel that it is your duty to sell the good books that no one else wants to sell. . . . This industry doesn't need more bookstores selling study aid books, but it needs bookstores that sell good books. So I'm just doing what I feel needs to be done, not just for myself, but for the bookselling industry."

SCHOLARLY BOOKS AND POLITICAL FRAMING

Independent bookstores' emphasis on scholarly books is also informed by the strategy of political framing. Since choosing a book often equates to endorsing its ideas, book selection is effectively a creative act of idea endorsement and articulation. The scholarly books stocked by independent bookstores, therefore, function as a communication medium through which these bookstores can actively explore and express views and ideas they value. This unique expressional attribute of scholarly books thus transforms book selection into an act of social participation, which can be broadly understood as engaging in the exploration and articulation of views and ideas with social, public, or political significance. Several interviewees discussed how they used book selection as a means of communication and self-expression.

For example, the owner of an independent bookstore in Suzhou explained: "We stock books that reflect our personal views. . . . For example, I always put George Orwell's *1984* and *Animal Farm* on our recommended books table because we share their ideas on authority and authoritarianism and want our customers to read them." This owner also reflected on how stocking heavily scholarly books aligned with their motivation for becoming a bookseller: "Selling mainly 'scholarly books' isn't the most financially wise way of running a bookstore, for you don't make much money out of these books. But we stick with them in that this is not just about selling books and making money—it's also about expressing ourselves." The manager of a Beijing-based independent bookstore similarly stated: "On the one hand, we want to sell books that our customers like and want to buy. But on the other hand, we also want our books to serve as a platform for sharing our thoughts with our customers." These comments highlight how independent bookstores see inventory stocking not as a mere business necessity but as a deeply personal act of interaction and impacting. Instead of merely marketing products, they imbue book selection with personal insights, emotions, and beliefs. This approach distinguishes independent bookstores from other types of bookstores and appeals to customers who value personalized interactions and meaningful connections in their book-buying experiences.

Also noteworthy is the first interviewee's classification of George Orwell's two novels as scholarly books. Interestingly, they were not the only independent bookseller I interviewed who categorized serious political novels as scholarly books. For these individuals, what makes this genre scholarly is its political dimension. As the first interviewee explains, it is "the ideas on authority and authoritarianism" in Orwell's novels that motivate them to share these works with their customers.

This finding highlights an important fact about scholarly books and their significance for independent bookstores. Many independent bookstores seek to use bookselling as a means of influencing customers and the wider society on issues of social, public, or political significance. For them, scholarly books are particularly valuable because their intense intellectual content can shape readers' views on important social, public, or political debates. These books thus possess a unique symbolic power that enables bookstores stocking them to engage in meaningful social participation in ways that other types of books do not.

This unique symbolic power stems from two primary ways that scholarly books can generate and convey meanings when stocked and displayed by a bookstore. First, a scholarly book is an embodiment of the ideas it contains; therefore, stocking and recommending such a book amounts to endorsing its ideas. Second, the manner in which these idea-rich books are displayed can itself produce meaning. For example, the physical placement of a book within a bookshop—the shelf it occupies, the category under which it is placed, the name of the category, and the books displayed alongside it—can all carry and denote meanings. These meanings can align with or diverge from the book's own ideas. While the book's author creates the ideas contained in a book, the bookstore possesses a creative capacity to curate and display its book collections to generate additional meanings that reflect its own views and perspectives.

I discovered these interesting dynamics when observing an independent bookshop in Beijing. This bookstore was renowned for its high-quality book collections. On one occasion, my attention was drawn to the unique way books were organized in this store. Instead of grouping books by disciplines or genres, titles were arranged into thematic categories like "Chinese Social Issues," "Chinese Intellectuals," "History of Chinese Empires,"

"Law and Civilization," and "Great Western Thinkers," to name only a few. Each thematic category encompassed books from various disciplines and/or genres, but all titles were unified by the category's overarching theme. For instance, the "Chinese Intellectuals" section included both biographies of prominent Chinese intellectuals and books written by them, whereas the "History of Chinese Empires" category featured a mix of history monographs and serious general-interest books about individual emperors and statesmen.

This thematic categorization and naming of inventory is a highly creative process. It allows the bookstore to guide its customers to read relevant books through its own interpretations of them. For example, readers might naturally perceive books under the label of "Great Western Thinkers" as embodying valuable ideas while reading those in the "Chinese Social Issues" category with a critical lens. Such thematic categorization thus subtly conveys meanings and perspectives, showing that book selection and display at independent bookstores are not neutral acts but deliberate forms of communication and even manipulation. In situations where certain topics cannot be explicitly discussed, this approach offers a tactical way of expression.

Figure 4.1 shows a bookcase in the aforementioned independent bookstore that is divided into three thematic sections entitled "宪政" (constitutionalism), "自由" (freedom), and "民主" (democracy). These concepts, laden with complex and often conflicting political connotations, lend themselves to political framing; that is, they are perfect for bookstores seeking to cultivate a distinctive political atmosphere to attract customers. This atmosphere stems not only from the specific books displayed under these themes but also from the aesthetic tools employed to draw customers' attention to them—such as the prominent bookshelf labels shown in figure 4.1.

FIGURE 4.1 Bookcase in an independent bookstore
Source: Author

As can be seen in figure 4.1, these labels are approximately the height of a standard 145×210 mm book and 70 cm in length—significantly larger than the standard yellow labels on the vertical bookcase behind them and, hence, more visible. Moreover, their dark background with crisp white font creates a high-contrast and legible design, which also imparts a somber aesthetic feel. These oversized labels thus serve to not only enhance visibility but also underscore the importance of the themes they represent. Through such displays, the bookstore conveys a clear message to its customers: These topics and books are important. Therefore, by combining a politicized thematic categorization of books and a display strategy highlighting this political dimension, this bookstore strategically imbues its space with a distinctive, politically evocative atmosphere.

This innovative use of scholarly books to harness their symbolic power to convey political meanings was not observed in nonindependent bookstores and was only seen in a few independent bookstores I visited. In other words, it is not a widely adopted practice, even among independent bookstores. Yet for those that do adopt it, the rewards can be high. For example, the bookstore discussed above is widely regarded as one of the best independent bookstores in China. It was also one of the few independent bookstores I studied that could achieve profitability from book sales alone, thanks to its highly original, and successful, approach to inventory selection and management. From this perspective, while political framing allows bookstores to engage in meaningful social participation, for most bookstores adopting it in book selection, this strategy serves primarily to deliver economic rather than political objectives. Elsewhere, I developed the concept of cultural politics to distinguish this approach from kind of the political activism often associated with independent bookstores and similar cultural institutions in other societies.[5] I argued that unlike activism, which aims at evoking grievance and instigating rebellion, cultural politics as practiced by Chinese independent bookstores through political framing is far less politically motivated.[6] Instead, it focuses on creating spaces—physical and intellectual—where polemical questions can be asked, alternative ideas explored, and diverse voices expressed. Therefore, it is an intellectual rather than political endeavor, which also serves the economic function of differentiating an independent bookstore from its competitors.

Rejecting "Popular Books": An Act of Cultural Distinguishing

Another common stocking strategy adopted by all the independent bookstores I studied was avoiding what they called "popular books." While there is no strict definition of this term, it generally refers to books or genres that tend to sell in large quantities, such as children's books, self-help guides, teen fiction, and similar genres. Particularly, all interviewees unanimously identified study aid books, or *jiaofu shu*, as the quintessential example of popular books they steadfastly excluded from their inventory. Why?

As noted in chapter 1, study aid books and school textbooks represent the largest submarket in the Chinese book industry, accounting for 20 percent of all books published and 40 percent of all printed books in 2014, for example.[7] These two categories are particularly lucrative for large retailers like Xinhua Bookstore, which relies heavily on these books for revenue. While school textbooks are primarily distributed through Xinhua Bookstores, study aid books are also widely retailed by privately owned bookstores. One study once estimated that over 80 percent of China's privately owned bookstores depended on these books for their survival.[8] I became acutely aware of the popularity of study aid books during a visit to a major book wholesale center in Beijing, where I discovered that more than two-thirds of the wholesalers trading there exclusively dealt with study aid books. Considering that most small- and medium-sized privately owned bookstores stock books from such local wholesalers, the composition of wholesalers at this specific wholesale center offers compelling evidence of the dominance of study aid books in the Chinese book retailing market.

The popularity of study aid books drives independent bookstores to avoid them so they can differentiate themselves from bookstores heavily stocking such titles. As one interviewee, the owner of a small independent bookstore in Nanjing, put it: "If I sold the same study aid books as those ordinary bookstores, what's the difference between me and them? I'd just become one of them and no longer an independent bookstore." This comment highlights how some independent bookstores link their rejection of popular books to identity-building.

Others avoid popular books because they genuinely consider these books beneath the cultural standards they uphold. More than one interviewee explained to me how they saw study aid books as inherently culturally inadequate, even inferior. As one bookstore owner said: "I don't sell study aid books because they are not high-quality books. I will never sell books I consider unworthy, however profitable they might be. . . . This is what makes me an independent bookseller: I'm here to help my customers find great books, books beneficial to them, not to become rich myself." This perception of study aid books as inferior in quality was widespread among the independent booksellers I interviewed. But where does this view come from?

First, many independent booksellers criticize study aid books for their practicality. They argue that these books promote rote learning and fail to foster creativity or critical thinking in students. Others contend that the popularity of study aid books reflects an overemphasis by schools and parents on academic achievement. Such overemphasis, they suggest, can hinder the development of well-rounded individuals and perpetuate a utilitarian culture focused on short-term, measurable results, such as exam success, rather than broader educational growth. Still others criticize study aid books for their perceived lack of cultural depth, failing to recognize that these books are not designed to offer cultural or aesthetic value but are intended for improving learning through systematic and repetitive practice.

Distinctly one-sided, these criticisms were prevalent among the independent booksellers I interviewed and were repeatedly cited as their rationale for not stocking study aid books. On the one hand, the criticism of study aid books' lack of cultural depth suggests that independent bookstores' rejection of these books—as well as other popular books—is rooted in a deep sense of cultural elitism: For these bookstores, books must possess significant cultural, artistic, or intellectual value to be deemed worthy. While this elitism is also evident in these bookstores' preference for scholarly books, it is most pronounced in their rejection of popular books, which they dismiss because of their association with ordinary bookstores.

On the other hand, independent bookstores' rejection of popular books is also motivated by their desire to differentiate themselves from mainstream bookstores, that is, a form of cultural distinguishing. While this distinction is not always perceived positively by everyone—pejorative terms like *pretentious* are often used by competitors to describe independent bookstores—it is effective in attracting target customers for these bookstores: generous individuals who seek cultural distinction by patronizing these culturally elevated institutions. Since any financial losses from low book sales due to avoiding popular genres can often be offset by the sale of other more expensive goods, the rejection of popular books also serves calculated fiscal objectives as well as cultural ones.

HOSTING EVENTS

Hosting various cultural events has become an integral part of many brick-and-mortar bookstores worldwide. According to Miller, in the United States, the history of bookstore events dates back to the 1910s, beginning when the Chicago-based department store Marshall Field introduced autographing parties in their stores to attract customers. Although the initial allure of these "innovative and glamorous" gatherings had declined by the middle of the century, the practice of bookstore events was later revived by independent bookstores in the 1970s.⁹ Since then, hosting events has become a more or less standard practice for bookstores across the United States.

Today, both independent and chain bookstores regularly organize various kinds of events to promote book sales. As Miller points out, the main purpose of bookstore events is to drive book sales—which is why bookstores typically refer to them as promotions.¹⁰ To better attract customers and boost book sales, US bookstores have been seen to host what Miller describes as "carnivalesque events."¹¹ Dress-up parties, animal performances, circuses, clowns, and magicians have all appeared in US bookstores to entice customers, and these events are experienced by customers as both promotion and entertainment. Events, therefore, play a dual role in American bookstores—promotional and entertaining.

For other bookstores, especially the independents, events serve an additional purpose: fostering community bonds. Activities like author tours, storytelling hours, reading groups, tea parties, raffles, and workshops help to transform these bookstores into "community centers."¹² Although these community-focused events also contribute to book sales, their primary purpose is to enable the bookstores to cultivate enduring customer relationships to ensure lasting book sales over time rather than relying on occasional bursts of sales created by carnivalesque extravaganzas.

Whether driven by promotional, entertaining, or community-building purposes, the way that bookstores organize events reflects their perceived roles and values in society. As book retailers, they organize entertaining events to attract customers and boost book sales. As community institutions, they host events to serve the local community. From this perspective, we can say that a bookstore's approach to hosting events reveals much about its self-identity and aspirations.

As such, it is unsurprising that Chinese independent bookstores are driven by different motives from their US counterparts when it comes to event curation. First, the promotional function of events holds less relevance for them. Several interviewees shared that they did not host events like author tours because they found these events to have little impact on driving book sales. One bookstore owner explained that publisher support, such as additional discounts, is critical for successful promotional events. Without this support, events alone rarely yield significant sales. However, publishers often prefer to work with larger bookstores rather than independents to promote new books, leaving most independent bookstores without the resources necessary for successful promotional book events. Reflecting on their experience, one interviewee remarked, "We hosted many such 'bookselling' events when we first opened, assuming that they'd bring in a lot of sales. After a while, we realized that wasn't the case. . . . Despite the resources we invested in organizing these events, we weren't really selling many more books. So we stopped doing it because it's not worth it."

Second, the community-bonding function of events is also largely irrelevant to Chinese independent bookstores. As previously noted, the notion of being rooted in and serving the local community—a defining feature of independent bookstores in the United Kingdom and the United States—is absent from the Chinese definition of independent bookstores. While some independent bookstores do cater to clientele with shared social and cultural interests, these social groups do not equal to communities in the geographic sense, nor do they perceive themselves as community institutions in the same way as their Western counterparts. As a result, among all the independent bookstores I studied, only one—which happened to be located in a large residential complex, known as *xiaoqu* in China—regularly hosted events aimed at serving residents living in or near its *xiaoqu*. None of the other independent bookstores associated their events with community-building purposes. If neither promotional nor community-bonding objectives register, then what drives Chinese independent bookstores to organize events?

Generally speaking, China's independent bookstores typically host two types of events: those that are free and open to all and those that require a fee to attend. Among the free events, talks are the most common, with nearly all the independent bookstores I studied having hosted such events. These talks can mix with other elements—such as book signing—to turn into other events (e.g., book launches). Most book launches are initiated and sponsored by publishers, whereas "talks not related to a specific book," as one interviewee put it, are often organized by the bookstores themselves.

"There are two main ways of organizing an event," explained the manager of a medium-sized independent bookstore in Beijing. This bookstore typically hosts more than one hundred events every year. "The first involves publishers approaching us to launch new books. In these cases, we would first evaluate the book's quality and only accept those that meet our standards. . . . We normally request publishers to provide complimentary copies instead of charging a venue fee." For self-organized events, according to this manager, the bookstore usually covers the speaker's travel and accommodation expenses but does not normally pay them for the talk. Importantly, this manager emphasized: "We keep both types of events free of charge to our customers."

In addition to talks, other popular free bookstore events include exhibitions, concerts, and performances. These events are offered free of charge often because the bookstore hosts them in order to support the artists, who need a platform to showcase their works but struggle to find suitable venues, rather than hoping to profit from the events. One interviewee who manages a film-themed independent bookstore described how they use their store to host exhibitions by young photographers: "We receive many applications from photographers to hold exhibitions in our store. Some are well-established, but we made the decision to support young photographers, even students, instead of doing commercial shows. . . . Since we don't charge for using our space, we can select the best photographers and showcase their best works."

Participatory events such as courses, workshops, reading groups, film nights, and so on tend to be fee-based. The fee charged can vary significantly across bookstores and events, ranging from a nominal amount to annual VIP subscriptions costing several hundreds of yuan. One bookstore owner explained to me the rationale for charging a small fee for their art workshops: "All our book-related events are completely free to attend. The workshops are run by a group of volunteers who want to promote traditional Chinese culture. We charge 30 yuan per participant per workshop; of this, 10 yuan is paid to the teacher, 10 yuan goes to the organizer for covering their administrative costs, and 10 yuan is retained by us to cover our hosting expenses. For only 30 yuan, a participant receives two hours of expert instruction in calligraphy, Guqin, or tea art. I think this is terrific value for money, a win-win for everyone involved."

Similar events at other bookstores often follow a comparable model: organized by third parties, such as nonprofit groups or hobbyist volunteers seeking a venue for their activities, rather than by the bookstores themselves. These events are usually open to anyone willing to pay a nominal fee to participate, which helps cover the basic costs of organizing the event and maintain its quality by limiting attendance. None of the bookstores

I studied considered these fee-based events a revenue stream. The only exception is when some bookstores host corporate functions, such as company celebration parties, for which they usually charge a large service fee. But these events represent a separate venue-hire service offered by some large independent bookstores purely for revenue generation and are not the kind of bookstore events I discuss here. Then, what drives these independent bookstores to host their public-facing events?

First, events remain one of the most effective ways to attract large numbers of customers to a bookstore. While the extent to which this increased traffic can translate into more sales and profits is a separate matter, for most bookstores, "it's always good to look busy," as one interviewee candidly put it. For mall-based independent bookstores receiving discounted rent from their landlords (i.e., the malls), hosting regular events to draw customers to the malls is often a contractual obligation. I discuss this in more detail in chapter 5.

This motivation to organize events, however, is not unique to independent bookstores but is widely shared by nonindependent bookshops as well. Therefore, a more nuanced analysis of what specifically motivates independent bookstores to organize their events is needed. In particular, it entails considering these bookstores' self-perceived roles and values in society. As discussed in chapter 3, many independent bookstores hold a distinct educational vision, seeing it as their duty to provide customers with intellectually uplifting reading materials. While this moral vision and the associated moral positioning strategy shape independent bookstores' book selection practices, they also impact how they curate events. Influenced by their vision to inform and even edify the public, some independent bookstores go beyond the standard author talks to host lectures and seminars, aiming to offer customers a more immersive intellectual experience. Such events need not be tied to a specific book but function mainly as open platforms for diffusing knowledge and sharing ideas.

This moral vision of facilitating public expression and circulation of ideas can sometimes take on a political dimension to produce political effects. An example is when politically controversial figures are invited to give talks in an independent bookstore. Even if the talks' topics are unrelated to politics, the appearances of these figures in the bookstore can generate political meanings and evoke a politically charged ambiance. At the very least, it signals to the public that the bookstore is a space for diverse viewpoints—a message resonating with many. In this sense, besides moral positioning, the strategy of political framing influences some independent bookstores' event-hosting practices.

However, playing the political card requires caution. Most bookstores navigate this terrain carefully, trying to strike a balance between cultivating a reputation as independent-minded booksellers and the risk of crossing political lines. Only a few bookstores act differently. For example, the owner of a small independent bookshop explained to me their motivation for hosting a popular but controversial public lecture series. This series often featured politically sensitive figures and hence created tensions with regulators. After being asked to cancel an event featuring a law-breaking speaker, this interviewee decided to end this series altogether.

AUTHOR: So you are banned from hosting events?

BOOKSELLER: Not exactly—it depends on the nature of the event. But I'm not interested in those ordinary *xiaozi* events where you talk about culture, arts, music, etc.[13] I only want to do events that no other bookstores can do.

AUTHOR: Why?

BOOKSELLER: I think a bookstore should be a public platform for expressing, discussing, and debating ideas, like a window to new ideas and perspectives. That's why we developed our lecture series. By hosting these lectures, we wanted to provide our customers with a forum to encounter different ideas and to think critically. Society needs such platforms, and they should be open to everyone. That's why we made our lectures free and open to all. . . . The speakers we invited were all famous scholars, and their ideas were incredibly valuable. That's why the lectures were so popular among our customers.

This interviewee represents a very small minority of independent booksellers who are explicitly driven by political goals, as opposed to by the strategy of political framing. They closely link bookselling with promoting confrontational political activism, using events and their bookstore to diffuse alternative and often illegal views and remarks. This approach sets them apart from the majority of independent bookstores, which, as I have reiterated throughout this book, employ political framing—and other culturally adapted strategies—as a competition strategy.

Finally, the strategy of cultural distinguishing also influences why and how independent bookstores host culture-themed events. The free talks, lectures, exhibitions, performances, and so on serve to further complement the rich cultural atmosphere these bookstores cultivate through their carefully curated book collections. Meanwhile, the fee-based events serve to attract customers with similar cultural tastes and socio-economic backgrounds, catering to their desire to socialize within their self-perceived elevated social echelons. These events thus fulfill these individuals' need to attain a sense of exclusivity and distinction through consumption.

DECORATING STORES

In the age of online retailing, attracting and retaining customers and converting increased foot traffic into purchases is essential to the survival and success of brick-and-mortar businesses. While this ability is critical to all types of physical retailers, it is particularly important for bookstores in that their main merchandise—books—are highly standardized products that customers can easily obtain online at significantly reduced prices. Unlike other physical retailers, where a customer might struggle to locate online the exact item they spotted in-store, bookstore customers can often effortlessly buy a book they found offline through a website. Amazon began its journey as an online bookstore for some good reasons. In sum, when it comes to the core function of book retailing, traditional brick-and-mortar bookstores can be easily replaced by their online counterparts.

However, despite their vulnerability to online bookstores, physical bookstores possess a distinct strength that affords them a competitive edge in today's e-commerce environment—their very physicality. Leveraging their ability to offer customers not only books but also an array of face-to-face services and experiences, many of these stores, once thought to be on the brink of extinction, have rebounded from the challenges of online book retailing. Central to this resurgence is these bookstores' strategic use of their physical spaces to create appealing and engaging cultural experiences that customers want to revisit and consume. In other words, by delivering value that online bookstores cannot replicate, physical bookstores have carved out a distinctive niche and have uncovered a formula for thriving in the digital age.

Not a New Story

Attracting customers through smart decor, a welcoming ambiance, and enhanced in-store facilities is not a new strategy bookstores use to bolster their appeal. In fact, the aesthetics and layout of a bookstore have long been recognized as critical factors affecting customer loyalty, and they continually innovate on store designs to stand out from competitors. In this regard, the evolution of independent bookstores in the United States and the United Kingdom throughout the twentieth century serves as a telling example.

According to Miller, prior to the emergence of mall-based chain bookstores in the 1960s, independent bookstores dominated the US bookselling market, serving mainly the affluent and intellectual clientele. However, despite their status as bastions of high culture, many of these early-day independents earned themselves a reputation for poor store management and were widely criticized for their "disorganized" stock, "erratic" store organization, and "dark and musty" environments.[14] Miller humorously remarks that many of these stores were so poorly designed and maintained that they seemed almost deliberately to distance themselves from customers by adopting narrow aisles, high shelves, and poor lighting.[15] Tim Coats, a veteran British bookseller, similarly recalls that many British independent bookshops in the 1980s were so derelict that they "looked like dump sites."[16] Miller concludes that independent bookstores' neglect of store environment not only alienated customers but also contributed to their decline against chains.

In contrast to independent bookstores, chain bookstores in the United States thrived during the 1960s and 1970s by prioritizing customer-friendly environments. Features like bright colors, good lighting, clear signage, wide aisles, and low shelves made browsing enjoyable and inviting, a stark departure from the sometimes intimidating atmosphere of independent bookstores.[17] By the 1980s and 1990s, book superstores further enhanced these features by introducing comfortable furniture to encourage customers to linger, relax, and socialize. In-store cafés and other amenities were also added to further cement the chain's advantage over the independent bookstore.

The success of chains and book superstores served as both a wake-up call and an inspiration for independent bookstores. Many began to upgrade their interiors and facilities, seeking to reestablish themselves not only as purveyors of exceptional books but also as providers of superior shopping experiences. Consequently, transforming bookstores into welcoming sanctuaries for book lovers has since become somewhat of a norm in the industry. A notable example of this trend was the relocation of the popular British independent bookstore, Foyles, to a new multilevel building in central London in 2015. "Designed to be light and airy," this new flagship store featured not only an expansive book collection but also a café, gift shop, and gallery, symbolizing the metamorphosis of a century-old bookstore into a modern cultural destination.[18]

The design of a bookstore's physical space, therefore, holds economic significance because it influences whether customers feel enticed or deterred by the store. However, beyond shaping customer relationships, a bookstore's visual presentation can also be a vehicle of meaning-making and expression. Through carefully curated book collections, decorations, furnishings, and facilities, a bookstore can craft and convey meanings and messages reflecting its values, identity, and attitudes. By revealing a bookstore's deeper aspirations, such nonverbal communication turns its physical space into a cultural statement, not merely a commercial site.

Space-Making by Independent Bookstores

Three practices are characteristic of Chinese independent bookstores' approach to store design. In contrast to nonindependent bookstores, many independent bookstores (a) are tastefully designed and decorated, (b) evoke a distinct Western culture ambiance, and (c) routinely use decorative artifacts to embed and convey political meanings and messages.

STORE DECOR AND CULTURAL DISTINGUISHING

When independent bookstores first appeared in the mid to late 2000s to be collectively perceived as a new type of bookstore, differing from both the state-owned Xinhua Bookstores and traditional privately owned bookstores, their tasteful decor served as an important distinguishing feature. It was such a novel development that it effectively symbolized the birth of a new species of bookstore. Since a bookstore's decor is often the first thing customers notice before they encounter the books, it plays a crucial role in shaping their first impression.

When O2Sun Bookstore, a harbinger independent bookstore, opened its doors in the early 2000s, it immediately captivated customers with its novel and attractive store design, which was unlike anything seen in other bookstores at the time. Among other things, it introduced bright, warm lighting augmented by ambiance lighting and table lamps, and soft furnishings to create a cozy, homelike atmosphere. Generous seating allowed customers to browse at their leisure, while wooden bookcases and tables were used to create a modern feel. This trendy appearance was completed by signage featuring modern fonts, bright colors, and English-language symbols.

While these design elements were innovative for bookstores at the time, they had been successfully applied in other retail contexts. Hence, when O2Sun Bookstore introduced them to book retailing, they were enthusiastically received by customers and quickly mimicked by other bookstores, especially the emerging independents. Therefore, although operating as a chain (it had over thirty branches in its heyday) and collapsing overnight in 2011 due to poor management, O2Sun Bookstore was and still is widely heralded as a pioneering independent bookstore, with its most important legacy being spearheading the practice of designing bookstores to offer not only quality books but also exceptional shopping experiences.

In the decade following O2Sun's demise, these principles were widely adopted and further developed by other independent bookstores. Today, most independent bookstores in China are tastefully designed and decorated—some can even be described as extravagant. Their aesthetic store design was once so distinctive and original that it served as a hallmark that differentiated independents from other types of bookstores. Although many Xinhua Bookstores and some nonindependent privately owned bookstores have since adopted similar practices and created some beautiful spaces, independent bookstores continue to lead in delivering an unparalleled book-shopping experience by blending outstanding literature with transcendent store environments.

A common strategy used by independent bookstores to achieve a stylish and sophisticated atmosphere is embedding Western cultural elements into their interior decor. Two stand out as particularly popular: the English language and images of Western cultural, literary, and intellectual figures. With regard to the use of the English language and symbols in interior design, almost every independent bookstore I visited displayed the English translation of their store name alongside the Chinese one to diffuse a contemporary ambiance. If the store also had a slogan, this was often translated into English and placed alongside the Chinese text. Moreover, English was widely used in store signage, café menus, and other textual contexts.

Figure 4.2 shows the entrance to a popular independent bookstore in Nanjing. Remarkably, this store chooses to display the French, rather than English, translation of its brand name—Librairie Avant-Garde—alongside the Chinese text on its imposing storefront to further accentuate its Western culture link. Similarly, figure 4.3 shows the exterior of an independent bookstore called Hugo Bookshop. It takes its name from the renowned French writer Victor Hugo (whose image also appears on the storefront—first from the left), and it prominently displays its slogan in both Chinese and English on the storefront, reading "獨立思考/Thinking Independently, 閱讀經典/Reading the Classic."

FIGURE 4.2 The bilingual shop front of an independent bookstore

Source: Author

FIGURE 4.3 Hugo Bookshop
Source: Author

Apart from featuring the English language and symbols in their interior design, many independent bookstores construct a Western culture ambiance by decorating their walls with pictures of famous Western writers, artists, or intellectuals. This practice was so ubiquitous that, soon after I started my fieldwork, I found myself losing count of how many times I encountered yet another picture of Ernest Hemingway or Oscar Wilde in the independent bookstores I visited! The pictures displayed were so similar that it seemed as if all these stores were designed by the same company. But of course, this trend was more of a result of emulation: Some popular independent bookstores pioneered this design, and others followed suit, leading to a remarkable proliferation of images of Western cultural, literary, or intellectual icons in Chinese independent bookstores.

Figures 4.4 and 4.5 were taken in two such popular independent bookstores, one in Nanjing and the other in Beijing. In figure 4.4, large black-and-white posters of renowned Western writers—including Albert Camus, Ernest Hemingway, and Franz Kafka—are hung on the walls along the gently sloping hallway leading to the center of the bookstore. These posters, combined with the striking black cross at the end of the hallway and a large picture of a music band—possibly The Rolling Stones—on the ceiling, create an imposing and unmistakable Western cultural ambiance. If not knowing it, one could easily mistake this scene for a bookstore in London or New York.

FIGURE 4.4 Inside of an independent bookstore in Nanjing

Source: Author

FIGURE 4.5 Inside of an independent bookstore in Beijing
Source: Author

Similarly, figure 4.5 shows a picture wall in another popular independent bookstore, which is covered with a collage of images of prominent Western cultural, literary, and intellectual figures, including Pierre Bourdieu (a sociologist), Jean-Paul Sartre (a philosopher), Franz Kafka (a writer), Andy Warhol (an artist), and Jim Morrison (a musician), among others. Notably absent from this collage is any image of a Chinese person. This conspicuous omission of figures from non-Western worlds showcases this bookstore's deliberate effort to curate a Western cultural vibe to highlight its link to and preference for Western culture.

By prominently displaying Western cultural symbols, independent bookstores construct a distinct Western atmosphere that differentiates them from other types of bookstores in China. I didn't encounter these design elements in any of the Xinhua Bookstores or nonindependent privately owned bookstores I visited. This link to Western culture, therefore, serves as a key differentiator that sets independent bookstores apart from their competitors. Moreover, just as tasteful store decor both visually differentiates and culturally distinguishes these bookstores, the Western cultural ambiance also adds an aura of cultural sophistication. Many Chinese people still associate Western culture with refined tastes, seeing familiarity with and appreciation for it as markers of social status. Therefore, by establishing and accentuating their links to Western culture, independent bookstores appear to target a particular demographic—affluent individuals seeking a sense of cultural distinction through engagement with the "high-brow" Western culture.

STORE DECOR AND POLITICAL FRAMING

Independent bookstores' pursuit of a Western cultural ambiance also aligns with the strategy of political framing. By emphasizing their Western cultural influences, they signal a deliberate distancing from Chinese culture, especially the official, state-sanctioned mainstream culture. This departure serves two key purposes. First, it supports their goal of detaching culture from political influences and reinstating culture's central and autonomous role in cultural production. In previous pages, we have seen how this stance shapes how independent bookstores select books and host events. It is therefore unsurprising that it also influences how they design and decorate their stores, transforming their interiors into another creative medium for embedding and conveying meaning. Second, it facilitates these bookstores' objective of differentiating themselves from competitors by positioning themselves as maverick—or even recalcitrant—players in the Chinese bookselling field. By adopting a cultural stance that not only diverges from mainstream norms but also privileges Western ideals, independent bookstores assert their distinction from both the state-owned Xinhua Bookstores and nonindependent privately owned bookstores.

The strategy of political framing is most evident in how some independent bookstores use decorative artifacts to embed and convey political meanings and messages. Although this practice is not as widespread as the other two design strategies and was observed only in a handful of independent bookstores, it is nonetheless important to understand. Not only is it unique to independent bookstores, but it also reflects their ambition to engage in wider social, public, or political participation. Much like their emphasis on promoting scholarly books and hosting communication-centered cultural events, the practice of using decorations to generate and convey political meanings showcases these bookstores' desire to serve as social hubs for diverse views and ideas.

Figures 4.6 and 4.7 show an artifact displayed in an independent bookstore. Made out of an old bird cage containing a piece of paper inscribed with the Chinese and English words for *power*, this artifact is a visual representation of the famous political slogan, "Put power in a cage." This phrase originates from a 2013 speech by President Xi Jinping to the party's Central Commission for Discipline Inspection. In it, President Xi stressed the importance of regulating the use of power to combat corruption, stating, "Power must be confined within an institutional cage, so as to create punitive mechanisms which make people dare not be corrupt, which prevent them from being corrupt, and which eliminate their desire to be corrupt."[19] This powerful statement was then distilled into the succinct slogan, "Put power in a cage," which quickly gained popularity among Chinese netizens, for it resonated with their shared desire to curb corruption by restricting the abuse of power. The phrase subsequently became a popular political expression in China.

As the slogan gained traction, however, it also acquired additional connotations. In popular usage today, it is often interpreted

FIGURE 4.6 A "Put power in a cage" artifact
Source: Erxi Liu

FIGURE 4.7 A "Put power in a cage" artifact
Source: Erxi Liu

as putting limits not only on bureaucratic abuse of power but also on political power in general. Advocates of this interpretation argue that what needs addressing is not only officials' misuse of power but also the pervasive reach of political power as a whole, both within and beyond political domains. This interpretation departs from the phrase's original emphasis on the party's internal mechanisms for preventing corruption by rendering a broader critique of political power in general. Such broad reading, therefore, diverges from and conflicts with the initial premise of reinforcing the party's leadership across all facets of governance, including the judiciary and law enforcement. Yet it has become very common in the everyday usage of this statement.

It is against this backdrop that the display of this artifact in the bookstore is intriguing. By prominently displaying this object, the bookstore owner signals their personal views on both combating corruption and limiting political power more generally. Although the owner initially downplayed the significance of this artifact when asked about their motivation for making and displaying it, saying they "just wanted to make something fun" out of a discarded bird cage, they eventually acknowledged that "an independent bookstore should have its own attitude on social issues and engage in social participation" and cited this as a reason for deciding to display it in the store after making it at home. From this perspective, the artifact's display is clearly underlain by politically related considerations.

Meanwhile, even if the owner had no intention of using this artifact to express their personal political stance, the object itself possesses an inherent ability to evoke its viewers' reflections on the topic of what constitutes reasonable use of political power. A piece of paper bearing the word *power* trapped in a cage visually conveys a sense of power being restricted and confined, a notion resonating even with viewers unfamiliar with the slogan. This notion is further amplified by the choice of the Chinese word for *power*, 权力. Unlike the English word, which encompasses broader meanings such as strength or ability, the Chinese term 权力 predominantly denotes "power" and "authority," often carrying a distinct political connotation. This example, therefore, vividly illustrates the potency of visual arts as employed by independent bookstores, where artifacts and decor are often used as powerful tools for creative and sometimes political expression.

Figure 4.8 showcases another example of a bookstore using decorative artifacts to convey political messages. In this case, the eye-catching piece is a large banner (circled in the picture) bearing the slogan, "Achieving liberation through reading." The political connotation of this slogan rests on the word *liberation*, which suggests that the current state of affairs is one of confinement or even oppression and that reading can enable people to break free. We are accustomed to being told that reading good books can enrich, enlighten, and broaden one's mind. In this case,

FIGURE 4.8 An "Achieving liberation through reading" sign
Source: Houniao Bujuan

however, this bookstore asserts to its customers that reading can bring them liberation, implying that their minds are currently constrained and their spirits unfree. This is a bold and provocative political statement. Yet the slogan permeated this bookstore, appearing extensively on banners, posters, handwritten notes, signs, as well as the custom tote bags, T-shirts, and mugs bearing the store's brand sold in the store's nonbook merchandise section. The repeated display of this slogan consistently reinforces the message to every visitor to this bookstore. The resulting political atmosphere, therefore, is both intense and unmistakable, setting it apart not only from nonindependent bookstores but also from most other independent bookstores.

In this chapter, I examined how China's independent bookstores manage three key aspects of operating a physical bookstore: selecting books, hosting events, and decorating stores. I showed that by implementing the culturally adapted strategies of political framing, moral positioning, and cultural distinguishing, they have successfully constructed a unique identity and developed distinctive offerings that enable them to attract and retain loyal customers. I have argued that central to their approach is a deep-seated desire to detach culture from political influence to reassert culture's central and autonomous role in cultural production. That is, the interplay between cultural and political forces plays a central role in the development and deployment of these strategies. In the next chapter, I will examine how the interplay between cultural and commercial forces shapes independent bookstores' other practices. Specifically, I will demonstrate how, in their effort to remain independent from political influence by leveraging economic forces, these bookstores embraced commercialization and consequently encountered both anticipated successes and unexpected challenges along the way.

5

THE ECONOMICS OF INDEPENDENT BOOKSELLING

So far, I have concentrated on examining how the cultural visions of independent bookstores shape their activities. In this chapter, I shift my focus to exploring their economic dynamics—that is, how these bookstores, which are as much cultural enterprises as they are cultural institutions, navigate the key economic processes involved in bookselling and make pivotal business decisions to survive and compete. Understanding these dynamics is crucial because it reveals how independent bookstores balance their cultural commitment and market demands while pursuing their ultimate goal of retaining culture's central and autonomous role in cultural production. I argue that in this process, these bookstores diverge in their attitudes toward the market and commercialization. Some fully embrace these dynamics, while others resist them. In what follows, I first examine a major challenge facing most independent bookstores and significantly shaping their behavior—I call it the conundrum of bookselling—and then analyze the three major solutions these bookstores employ to overcome this challenge.

THE CONUNDRUM OF BOOKSELLING

Independent bookstores in China face a major challenge that threatens not only their financial viability but also their very identity as bookstores: They struggle to stock and sell books profitably. This challenge, which I call the conundrum of bookselling, was evident in nearly all of the independent bookstores I visited and studied. That is, it is a structural—or systemic—issue that affects the independent bookselling sector as a whole rather than only a few poorly managed shops. Understanding its causes and consequences, therefore, is crucial for grasping some key behaviors of independent bookstores.

The Problem of Stocking

Nearly all of the independent bookstore owners or managers I interviewed identified inefficient book stocking rather than a lack of customers or low sales as their primary obstacle to profitability. Many cited the lack of a stable and cost-efficient book supply as their biggest challenge, one they considered more challenging than competition from online bookstores. What causes this stocking problem? Why is it so difficult for independent bookstores to obtain stock efficiently? Which channels do they use, and why are they ineffective? To answer these questions, we need to revisit our earlier discussions of the book distribution and wholesale sectors in China and examine some key shifts in these sectors over the last two decades.

THE DECLINE OF LOCAL BOOK WHOLESALERS

As discussed in chapter 1, privately owned bookstores in China have traditionally relied on three main channels for stocking books. Large bookstores tend to procure books directly from publishers and/or large regional or national book distributors to secure better terms. Small- to medium-sized bookstores predominantly stock books from local book wholesalers based in book wholesale centers commonly found in most provincial capitals and some large noncapital cities. These wholesalers, supplied by large distributors and publishers, have historically played a critical role in supplying and supporting small bookstores. Throughout the 1990s and 2000s, these channels—that is, from publishers, large distributors, or small wholesalers—ensured efficient inventory acquisition for privately owned bookstores.

Starting in the late 2000s, this landscape began to shift, leaving many independent bookstores unable to source books through their usual means. A key change was the decline of local book wholesalers, which had long played a pivotal role in supplying small- and medium-sized bookstores, including most independent bookstores. Roughly from the mid-2000s, many local book wholesalers have closed down. When I visited a major book wholesale center in Beijing in 2014, more than 20 percent of its shops were vacant. This center was once home to more than three hundred wholesalers and was one of the largest book wholesale centers in northern China. As noted in chapter 1, a shop in a book wholesale center refers to an office space rented by a wholesaler to use as its store, office, and warehouse (see figure 1.3 for an example). According to one wholesaler who had traded in this center for over a decade, many of the vacant shops had been empty for years due to a lack of tenants. This wholesaler explained, "They can't get new companies in because the trend has been for us wholesalers to close down." During my fieldwork, I visited five book wholesale centers in five different cities. All five centers had experienced a 10 to 30 percent decline in the number of wholesalers, according to those still trading there. Although no official data exist to quantify the extent and impact of this trend, the testimonies of remaining wholesalers provide important insights into the scale of the decline of the local book wholesale sector since the mid-2000s.

This decline has not been uniform across subfields. As explained in chapter 1, most local book wholesalers specialize in particular types of books—for example, the wholesaler shown in figure 1.3 deals in exam books, a subset of educational books. My observations in the wholesale centers suggest that while wholesalers of educational and children's books had largely continued to thrive—they accounted for more than 70 percent of the remaining traders in those centers—wholesalers of literature and social science books (including scholarly books) have been hit the hardest. During my visits, shops specializing in these titles were noticeably quieter and carried far less stock than those bustling educational or children's book wholesalers. I had the opportunity to speak with the owner of one such shop in the Beijing center about his experience as an academic book wholesaler specializing in academic monographs:

> It has been like this for a while. As you can see, you're the only customer here. In the past, this time of day [11 A.M.] was our busiest. But today, so far I have received only one telephone order from a client in Tianjin. . . . Many academic book wholesalers have folded in the last few years. Most of those that have left [the name of this book wholesale center] were academic book wholesalers like us. Those selling children's books and study aid books haven't been affected much, for market demand for their books is still very high. We academic book wholesalers have lost a lot of clients because many bookstores selling these books have folded.

This remark highlights the link between the decline of local book wholesalers and the difficulties independent bookstores have in stocking books. Wholesalers dealing the types of books they prefer—academic monographs, serious nonfiction, and high-quality literature—are among those hit the hardest in the decline of the wholesale sector. As a result, both established and new independent bookstores are affected by a shortage of suppliers. The established ones would have lost longstanding suppliers, while many newly opened independents simply struggled to find any stable suppliers at all.

THE CHALLENGE OF STOCKING FROM PUBLISHERS

The difficulties in stocking books from local wholesalers push some independent bookstores to try to order directly from publishers. These are primarily the state-owned publishing houses because most privately owned book companies publishing collaboratively with state houses outsource distribution instead of handling it themselves. This option, however, has its own problems. As many independent bookstores have discovered, publishers are often reluctant to supply privately owned bookstores directly because establishing consignment contracts with these businesses is deemed risky. As discussed in chapter 1, publishers typically supply clients on consignment contracts. Under consignment, a bookstore pays only for sold copies and can return unsold stock to the publisher. In the past, some large- and medium-sized privately owned bookstores could trade with publishers on such terms by holding an account with them. Today, however, the publishers rarely open consignment-based accounts for privately owned bookstores, regardless of size, due to debt concerns if these stores were to fold unexpectedly.

Under the consignment system, publishers send books to clients without taking immediate payment. Payment is settled instead at the end of a designated invoice period, ranging from three to twenty-four months. The length of the period varies depending on factors like the type of client (e.g., longer for distributors and wholesalers than for retailers, and longer for Xinhua Bookstores than for other bookstores), the type of book (e.g., longer for academic books), and the order volume (e.g., shorter for online bookstores—usually three months—due to large order sizes). Trust and vouching mechanisms, therefore, play a critical role in the smooth functioning of this system. Publishers are more inclined to supply Xinhua Bookstores, for example, and offer favorable terms because, as state-owned enterprises, they are considered reliable. Similarly, large privately owned distributors and wholesalers are trusted thanks to their long-established relationships with publishers. In contrast, most privately owned bookstores are considered high-risk due to their lack of similar vouching mechanisms and greater likelihood of bad debt. For the same reason, most local book wholesalers—as small- or medium-sized privately owned businesses—tend to be supplied by distributors rather than by publishers.

A sales manager at a medium-sized publishing house explained why many publishers decided to stop supplying privately owned bookstores on consignment. "What if they place an order today and go out of business next week? What if the owner simply disappears, leaving you with a lot of unpaid debts and unreturned stock? This has happened to many publishers, including us, which was why we decided to stop opening new accounts for privately owned bookstores." This manager further noted that Xinhua Bookstores, being state-owned, are perceived as much more reliable and financially stable than privately owned bookstores, which "can go bankrupt in any minute." "As a publisher, the last thing you want to hear is a bookstore has closed down, the owner has vanished, and it's one of your clients." According to this manager, during the 2000s, following the rise of online bookstores, many privately owned bookstores quietly closed down without notifying their suppliers, leaving many publishers, distributors, and wholesalers with unpaid debts and unreturned stock. Many publishers thus incurred substantial losses. "Since then, as far as I know, nearly all state-owned publishing houses have stopped supplying privately owned bookstores. We still supply our existing private clients but no longer accept new ones."

Unable to obtain books on consignment, some independent bookstores have tried to purchase them in cash. Yet this approach is often impractical. Most publishers impose a minimum order threshold—based either on quantity or on total order value—that exceeds what most independent bookstores need and can afford. Publishers also typically implement a "no-return, no-exchange" policy for cash orders, leaving bookstores to absorb the risk of unsold inventory on their own. Lastly, publishers often prioritize fulfilling large orders from their primary clients—i.e., distributors, Xinhua Bookstores, and online retailers—over smaller orders from privately owned bookstores. This can result in substantial delays, sometimes up to several weeks, in receiving stock. At a time when most books are only a click away from readers, such delays can significantly impact a bookstore's sales. One Beijing-based independent bookstore—among the few I studied that managed to secure direct supply from publishers—addressed this issue by operating a dedicated order-collection team. The team, comprising a driver and a van, collected stock daily from publisher warehouses in Beijing and nearby areas. "Our driver goes out every day to collect orders from the publishers," said the buying director of this bookstore. "He is one of our busiest, and his work is absolutely vital because collecting orders can save us at least two days' lead time."

THE PROBLEM WITH STOCKING ONLINE

Due to the shortcomings of stocking from local book wholesalers and publishers, many independent bookstores have turned to the internet for solutions. Nearly all of the independent bookstores I studied reported having purchased books from the large online bookselling websites—Dangdang, JD.com, and Tmall Books—for resale in their stores at least once. About a quarter of these bookstores—mostly small or newly opened ones—reported that they relied entirely on these platforms for stocking, while others regularly supplemented their main supplies with online purchases. In short, online stocking has become an important stocking channel for independent bookstores, and it offers two main advantages: faster delivery and steeper discounts. Major platforms like Dangdang, JD.com, and Tmall Books offer next-day or same-day delivery, making ordering from them often quicker than other stocking channels available to the independents. Moreover, these platforms regularly hold special sales events where books can be purchased at significantly reduced prices, typically at 50–70 percent off the list price, far surpassing the usual discounts offered to independent bookstores by local book wholesalers at 28–35 percent.

However, online stocking has its drawbacks. The special sales, while economical, are sporadic, and book prices outside these periods may not be as competitive. Moreover, availability during these sales can be unstable, with purchasing limits often imposed (e.g., a maximum of two copies per account). More important, bookstores relying on online stocking risk subjecting their book selection to the preferences of these large platforms, which clearly prioritize popular and commercial titles over the kinds of quality books independent bookstores aspire to offer.

As a result, although online stocking has become an important channel for independent bookstores, it is not a comprehensive solution to their stocking challenges. Consequently, most independent bookstores I studied reported having varying degrees of difficulty in obtaining stock and expressed dissatisfaction with their inventory size and turnover rate. For example, many small or newly opened independent bookstores I visited carried only a few hundred titles, while an inventory of over three thousand titles was considered decent by most interviewees. Yet it remains a threshold out of reach for many. Meanwhile, most independent bookstores have a low inventory turnover rate (it refers to how frequently new stock arrives). Several interviewees pointed out that high turnover creates a sense of freshness and is crucial for attracting and retaining customers. However, most independent bookstores struggle to replenish their stocks as frequently as they desire. As one owner of a small yet well-stocked bookstore (around seven thousand titles) said, "Ideally, I'd love to have new stock coming in every day to keep things fresh for our customers. But the best I can achieve at the moment is getting deliveries every five to seven days, which amounts to sixty to seventy new titles per month." Most independent bookstores I visited had a much smaller inventory and lower turnover rate than this bookstore, demonstrating the severity and pervasiveness of the challenge of stocking across this sector.

The Struggle to Make a Profit

Despite their challenges in obtaining stock, most independent bookstores will eventually manage to acquire some books to sell in their stores. They are then confronted with another and perhaps more challenging task—selling these books to make a profit. During my fieldwork, I found that most independent bookstores struggled to generate sufficient revenue from book sales to cover their basic operating costs. Like many retail businesses, the primary expenses for physical bookstores are rent and employee salaries. While in some large cities, high labor costs can surpass the rent, the majority identified high rent as their greatest hurdle to achieving profitability. "The rent eats up the profit," as one interviewee succinctly put it. The great disparity between high rent and modest revenue was illustrated to me by the owner of a small independent bookshop in a noncentral area of Beijing:

> My monthly rent is 20,000 yuan. To cover this, I need a daily profit of 660 yuan. Assuming that I have a 30 percent gross margin—which I don't because I sell most books at a 10 percent discount—I'd need to sell 2,200 yuan worth of books every day to make that 660 yuan of profit. Let's say each book is sold at 40 yuan, I must then sell at least 55 books a day. That, I can tell you, is impossible. I can usually sell 10–15 books on weekdays and a few more on weekends, but 55 books a day? That has never happened.

This testimony highlights the two primary causes of independent bookstores' low profit margins: the generally modest gross profit margins of bookselling and their low book sales. As noted earlier, independent bookstores typically receive a 28–35 percent discount from their suppliers, meaning that they can earn a gross profit of 28–35 percent if selling books at full price. However, since most independent bookstores sell books at a small discount—5 to 10 percent—the average gross profit margin reported by most independent bookstores I studied falls between 20 percent and 30 percent. As a gross profit margin, this figure may be narrow, but it is not low—many highly profitable businesses operate with even lower gross margins. This suggests that there are other factors contributing to independent bookstores' unprofitability in book sales.

The first factor may be the low book price in China. For example, the median price of a new book published in 2019 was only 45 yuan (approximately US$6.54). The second factor may be independent bookstores' low sales volume. Regarding the first factor, since it is difficult to meaningfully compare book prices across categories, it is hard to definitively conclude whether books are indeed underpriced relative to other goods to have resulted in independent bookstores' low profit margins. Moreover, since all bookstores adhere to the same recommended retail prices (RRP), independent bookstores' low profitability is more likely due to their low sales volume rather than book pricing in general.

On the one hand, most independent bookstores adopt an elitist approach to bookselling, selling mainly serious intellectual nonfiction (scholarly books) and high-quality literature while intentionally avoiding popular genres. While this approach helps to distinguish them from their competitors, it limits their sales potential due to the exclusive nature of their inventory. On the other hand, some interviewees attributed their low sales to competition from online bookstores. This view was especially popular among booksellers who opened their businesses before the rise of online bookstores. Drawing from their experiences in the preonline era and comparing their past and present sales, these booksellers tended to conclude that competition from online bookstores was the main driver of their declined sales. In contrast, newer booksellers often had a different perspective. Instead of blaming online bookstores, they tended to ascribe their low book sales to what they perceived as a small book-reading population in China. One interviewee remarked:

Online bookstores or not, it wouldn't make much difference to my business. Online bookselling has changed how and where people buy books, but not the number of people who read and buy books. If the overall demand for books is low, it doesn't matter who gets the bigger slice of the cake and who gets the smaller slice, for what really matters is the size of the cake. . . . Our problem is that we have a small cake. I don't blame online bookstores for taking our customers. On the contrary, I think online bookstores can help make the cake bigger by making book purchasing more affordable and convenient to attract more people to buy and read books.

Some statistics seem to support the argument that Chinese people do not read enough books to sustain a thriving bookselling market. According to a 2021 report by the Chinese Academy of Press and Publication (CAPP), the average Chinese adult reads 4.76 printed books and 3.30 e-books annually, spending just 21.05 minutes per day on reading printed books. This is significantly lower than the 68.42 minutes spent surfing the internet and the 101.12 minutes devoted to using mobile phones.[1] On the surface, these figures may suggest there is considerable room for increased book reading among Chinese adults. However, if we take into account China's large population—over 1.4 billion in 2024—whether the country's book-reading population can be described as small and whether this contributes to independent bookstores' low book sales are questions open to debate.

Still other interviewees suggested that rising book prices since the mid-2000s were another important factor causing their low book sales, for higher prices can deter customers from purchasing books at physical bookstores. A seasoned bookseller who had been in the business since the 2000s remarked: "Books are undoubtedly overpriced these days. Every day, I hear customers complaining about the high prices. We're losing customers because of this. More people will buy books online if they feel the prices are too high and believe they can save a lot of money by shopping online."

A buying director at a well-established independent bookstore in Beijing shared a similar view, drawing upon book price data they had been collecting since 2007. In an interview in 2017, this director shared with me that their data suggested an approximate 10 percent increase in book prices from 2007 to 2017. Since this store was a typical independent bookstore and had an inventory of more than seventy thousand titles, comprising mainly scholarly books and high-quality literature, its data should reflect wider trends in this sector. That is, we can reasonably conclude that, between the mid-2000s and the mid-2010s, the average price of books sold by a typical independent bookstore increased by about 10 percent. But how does this increase compare with other related indices, such as changes in the prices of other consumer goods and shifts in income levels?

Figure 5.1 compares this figure with changes in the consumer price index (CPI) and per capita disposable income from 2006 to 2015. It shows that the average book price increase consistently outpaced growth in disposable income (except in 2006 and 2007) and significantly surpassed CPI increases throughout the period. Taken together, these figures indicate that book price increases were notably steeper than changes in both disposable income and the general cost of living, suggesting their highly likely impact on consumers' book purchasing decisions. Indeed, according to a report by *China Publishing Today*, a leading trade journal for the book publishing industry, the average list price of a new literary book published in 2014 was 43.6 yuan.[2] In contrast, a 2015 survey by the Chinese Academy of Press and Publication revealed that the maximum price Chinese consumers

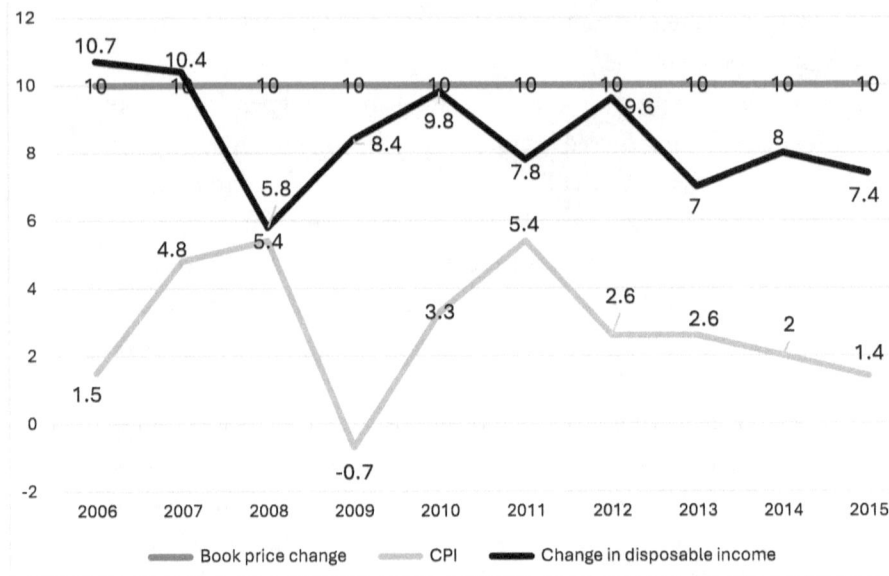

FIGURE 5.1 Changes in book price, Consumer Price Index (CPI), and disposable income per capita (%)

Source: National Bureau of Statistics of China (for CPI and disposable income)

were willing to pay for a new two-hundred-page literary book was only 20 yuan—less than half the average list price in 2014.[3] This significant gap between actual and anticipated book prices highlights the great potential impact of book prices on book purchasing decisions. It is plausible, as many independent booksellers reported, that the higher book price has driven consumers away from physical bookstores, including the independents.

What, then, drove the steep increases in book prices? As in other industries, book pricing is primarily influenced by two factors: production costs and projected profit margins. While rising paper prices and other increased production expenses played roles in book price hikes, most interviewees pointed to two other factors as the main drivers behind the significant rise in prices since the mid-2000s.

The first factor is the substantial reduction in initial print runs at most state-owned publishing houses since the 2000s. These reductions were reportedly implemented to control return rates, a key performance metric used by publishers to evaluate efficiency. It is calculated as the value of returned books divided by the value of books shipped or sold within a year. Since high return rates were commonly interpreted as signs of inefficiency during the sector-wide corporatization reforms of the 2000s (see chapter 1), to maintain a low return rate, many publishers chose to reduce the number of books they sent to clients, resulting in decreased print runs. A sales manager at a medium-sized publishing house explained: "Print runs have dropped significantly in the last ten years. Previously, ten thousand copies were standard for most of our new books. Today, it's five thousand copies for our priority projects and only two thousand to three thousand copies for other books." Smaller print runs necessarily increased the unit production cost, which, in turn, drove up RRP. Reduced print runs thus served as a cost-side factor causing book price hikes.

The second and perhaps more important factor identified by many interviewees was the large discounts publishers were forced to offer online retailers. According to this view, leveraging their market dominance, platforms like Dangdang and JD.com routinely demanded discounts so unreasonably deep that compliance tended to render publishers loss-making. However, since most publishers could not afford to lose online sales, they chose to increase their book prices to mitigate the impact of these high discounts on their overall profitability. A publisher-turned-bookseller explained this dynamic to me:

Suppose I publish a book priced at 20 yuan. Generally speaking, 30–35 percent of a book's price goes toward covering its production cost. Let's say it's 35 percent, then the cost of producing this book is 7 yuan. Another 20 percent of the price is the publisher's profit, so 4 yuan for this book. The remaining 9 yuan, or 45 percent of the price, is the margins reserved for distributors, wholesalers, and retailers. Therefore, 45 percent is the highest discount I can afford to offer to any distributors, wholesalers, or retailers. Now you have the online bookstores demanding a 70 percent discount. That is, they are only willing to pay 6 yuan for this book, leaving me with a margin of minus 1 yuan, meaning that I will lose money by selling the book at the current price. Obviously, no publisher would accept this but neither could they afford to say no to the large platforms. So in order to cover the 7 yuan production cost and retain the 4 yuan profit, I must raise the book's price to at least 37 yuan to accommodate the 70 percent discount demanded by the online bookstores. And this makes the same book 80 percent more expensive for consumers.

In this example, a 25 percent increase in the discount offered to online retailers results in a staggering 80 percent increase in the book's price, vividly illustrating the significant impact of steep discounts demanded by online bookstores on book pricing. While a 70 percent discount is rare (though not unheard of), a 50 percent discount—that is, only 5 percent higher than the typical 45 percent discount—is common. Even with this small adjustment, the publisher must raise the book's price from 20 to 22 yuan in order to cover the 7 yuan production cost and retain the 4 yuan profit, resulting in a 10 percent price increase. Coincidentally, this increase precisely aligns with the 10 percent average price hike observed by the aforementioned buying director. This example thus demonstrates how even a modest increase in discounts offered to online retailers (5 percent) can lead to substantial book price increases for consumers (10 percent), highlighting the link between rising book prices and the discounting practices of online retailers.

DIVERSIFYING INTO NONBOOK BUSINESSES

On Diversification

It should now be clear that the first defining feature of the economic condition of independent bookstores is their struggle to make a profit from their core business of bookselling. In other industries, if a company struggles in its primary business, chances are it will also face difficulties with diversification because while diversification may seem like an alluring option for struggling businesses, it is extremely difficult to execute well. Entering a new or seminew market with established players is not only unpredictable but also highly risky and can potentially jeopardize the company's core business if undertaken unwisely.[4]

Due to these high stakes, strategy professor Constantinos Markides advises that companies should approach diversification with caution, pursuing it only if specific criteria are met. The first criterion is that the company must possess "unique and unassailable competitive strengths," strengths that have already made the company successful in its current market and are crucial for success in the new market. These strengths must also be transferable to the new market to grant the company a significant competitive edge against incumbent players. Markides calls such strength a company's "strategic asset," defining it as what a company does better than its competitors.[5] After identifying its strategic assets, a company must then critically evaluate whether these strengths are as crucial for success in the new market as they are in the current one. Not all capabilities are universally valuable; what is essential in one industry may well be irrelevant in another. A company, therefore, should only consider diversification if its strategic assets are both transferable to and valued in the new market.

With this basic understanding of business diversification, we can now analyze the diversification strategies employed by independent bookstores and assess whether they are wise or not. One caveat is important, though: Unlike Markides, who examines diversification as a discrete business decision made by individual companies based on their unique circumstances, my analysis focuses on the collective pursuit of diversification by independent bookstores as a whole. This collective perspective is warranted by the widespread prevalence of diversification among independent bookstores in China—it is so prevalent that bookstores that exclusively sell books are rare. Moreover, these bookstores have employed some highly similar diversification strategies, suggesting that the driving forces behind their diversification are likely rooted in some shared, sectoral conditions rather than discrete circumstances of individual bookstores. A thorough understanding of this phenomenon thus requires analyzing diversification as a collective endeavor undertaken by the sector as a whole.

Given this perspective, we can now examine two questions to understand independent bookstores' diversification: What are these businesses' common strategic assets that justify their diversification choices, and what do they excel at in their core business of book retailing that makes them competitive in the new markets they diversify into?

In the previous chapters, we examined how independent bookstores employ three culturally adapted strategies to deliver unique values for customers and thereby secure competitive advantages over competitors. These advantages constitute their strategic assets. Specifically, these bookstores excel in two areas. First, independent bookstores possess a superior cultural profile. This stems primarily from their culturally discerning approach to bookselling, where they focus on selling high-quality intellectual and literary works while avoiding popular and commercial genres. Many further enhance their cultural appeal by hosting thoughtfully curated cultural events of various kinds. Second, many independent bookstores offer customers a unique experiential value through their aesthetically pleasing and inviting store environments. This value affords them a competitive edge not only among book retailers but also potentially over other retail businesses where aesthetic store environment is crucial for customer attraction. Together, these capabilities enable independent bookstores to deliver what Jean Baudrillard calls "sign value"—a distinct form of commodity value avidly pursued by status-conscious consumers seeking to enhance their social standing through the conspicuous consumption of goods or services that confer prestige.[6] It is by leveraging this strength that independent bookstores have developed their two primary diversification strategies: establishing in-store coffee shops or similar catering services and selling premium nonbook cultural merchandise.

"A Bookstore Is Incomplete Without a Coffee Shop": The Lure of the In-Store Coffee Shop

The term "coffee shop" is used here as an umbrella term to refer to the diverse range of catering services offered by independent bookstores, including tea houses, bars, cafés, restaurants, and more. All of these were encountered during my fieldwork, although the coffee shop was the most popular choice.

The history of bookstore-run coffee shops in China predates the advent of independent bookstores themselves. As early as the 1990s, some privately owned bookstores in large cities like Beijing and Shanghai were already integrating coffee shops or tea houses into their stores to offer customers simple beverages. However, the services were not for financial gain. Instead, they were offered primarily to bring convenience to customers. "We weren't thinking about making money when we first opened this tea house back in the 1990s," recalled the owner of an independent bookstore in Beijing. "We did so because we sensed that some customers needed a space in the bookstore to sit down with a book or to meet with friends. We set up the tea house to meet this need. Making more money wasn't a consideration, as we were making enough profits from selling books." Economic considerations, therefore, played only a secondary role in the emergence of the first generation of bookstore-run coffee shops in China. The services were generally viewed as valuable supplements to the bookstores' core bookselling business but did not hold any more significance.

Partly because of this light economic focus, the bookstore-run coffee shops of the 1990s were rudimentary in both the products they offered and their services. Typically tucked into a corner, situated on the first or second floor, or nestled in the backyard of the main bookstore, the facilities often comprised only a few tables and chairs. The menu was simple, too. For example, the above interviewee described to me how they used the kind of teapots "every household in China had back in those days" to make and serve tea to customers. "Nothing was fancy about it back then," recalled this bookseller. "Our main job was to look after the bookstore; the tea house was only something we did on the side."

THE ECONOMICS OF INDEPENDENT BOOKSELLING • 177

This light-touch approach to the in-store catering service, however, began to change dramatically in the following decades. The kinds of coffee shops, tea houses, cafés, and, in some cases, full-fledged restaurants run by independent bookstores today are worlds apart from their modest predecessors of the 1990s. During my fieldwork, I visited numerous independent bookstore-run coffee shops and was struck by the quality of both the products offered and the overall service provided. In many bookstores, the coffee shop occupied a prominent location, sometimes at the front of the store, to attract customers. In some instances, the coffee shop even took up more floor space than the book section to accommodate extensive furnishings and large numbers of patrons.

Figure 5.2 shows an independent bookstore where the attached coffee shop is so extensive that it effectively blends

FIGURE 5.2 Independent bookstore-run coffee shop where the coffee shop effectively blends into the book section

Source: Author

into the book section. This layout, however, inevitably hinders book browsing, for chairs and tables are placed against the bookshelves, making access to books cumbersome and inconvenient. Its adoption, therefore, illustrates the store's prioritization of the coffee shop business over bookselling. Similarly, figure 5.3 shows a much larger independent bookstore where the coffee shop dominates the entire ground floor, relegating the main bookstore to a narrow space on the first floor. This arrangement sends a clear message to customers: This is not just a bookstore but also a standalone coffee shop that welcomes everyone, whether they visit the store for books or coffee.

These developments highlight the transformed role of in-store coffee shops in today's independent bookstores. No longer considered auxiliary or supplementary, the coffee shop has become a core component of many independent bookstores and an indispensable part of their offerings to customers. This shift

FIGURE 5.3 Independent bookstore-run coffee shop where the coffee shop dominates the entire ground floor

Source: Author

is aptly captured by one interviewee: "A bookstore is incomplete without a coffee shop."

But what has driven these changes? The developments are a result of the growing financial importance of coffee shops for independent bookstores. For many, the coffee shop has become their financial lifeblood, contributing the majority of their revenue and profit. Among all the independent bookstores I studied that had an in-store coffee shop, most reported higher revenue from their catering services than from book sales. Approximately a quarter reported that book sales accounted for less than 30 percent of their total income. This percentage dwindles even further when it comes to profit margins, for books typically yield lower margins than coffee. When asked about their motivation for opening an in-store coffee shop, the manager of a medium-sized independent bookstore in Beijing responded candidly, "Because of the profit a coffee shop can generate. We make more money from selling 50,000 yuan worth of coffee than from selling 100,000 yuan of books. So the coffee shop is really important for us in business terms." This statement highlights that economic necessity drove the integration of coffee shops into independent bookstores.

The high profitability of in-store coffee shops can be attributed to coffee's high gross profit margin and high selling price in the Chinese market. According to the founder and CEO of a large coffee shop chain with more than eight hundred stores across China as of 2023, a cup of freshly brewed, shop-made coffee typically yields an impressive gross profit margin of 70–75 percent. This margin is consistent regardless of the coffee shop's size (be it a large chain or a small independent) and ownership structure (whether transnational brands like Starbucks or locally-run business). "This is why the coffee shop market is so competitive," the CEO remarked. "The gross profit margin indeed is quite high."

A 70–75 percent gross profit margin surpasses most independent bookstore's 20–30 percent gross margin in bookselling by an astounding 50 percent, highlighting the attraction of running an in-store coffee shop, especially for those facing financial difficulties. However, the high gross profit margin is only one factor. Equally important is the relatively high selling price of coffee and the rapid growth of China's coffee market.

Table 5.1 compares the prices of a Starbucks grande caffè latte in China and the United Kingdom in 2023 alongside the respective median household disposable incomes for each country in 2022. The data reveals a striking contrast. While the average UK consumer's annual disposable income could purchase up to 7,960 cups of this coffee, their Chinese counterpart could afford only 922 cups with their annual disposable income. This disparity shows that coffee prices in China can be considerably higher relative to consumer income than in other markets. The combination of coffee's high retail price and high gross profit margin, therefore, makes the coffee shop business highly lucrative in China. Because large national chains like Starbucks typically implement flat national pricing for their products and their prices are often used by other companies as pricing benchmarks, Starbucks' pricing provides a reliable indicator of the average

TABLE 5.1 COFFEE PRICES AND HOUSEHOLD DISPOSABLE INCOME IN THE UNITED KINGDOM AND CHINA

	United Kingdom	China
Starbucks grande cafè latte (SGCL)	4.05 GBP	34 RMB
Median household disposable income in 2022 (MHDI)	32,300 GBP	31,370 RMB
Ratio of SGCL to MHDI	1 : 7960	1 : 922

Source: UK office for national statistics; National Bureau of Statistics of China

price of freshly brewed, shop-made coffee in the Chinese market: between 20 and 40 yuan per cup.

The attraction of the coffee shop business is further reinforced by China's large and fast-growing coffee shop market. Here, it is important to distinguish between the *coffee shop market* and the broader *coffee market*. The latter encompasses various market segments categorized by product type, such as whole beans, instant coffee, ground coffee, and coffee pods or capsules, or by distribution channels, such as supermarkets, convenience stores, vending machines, and specialist retailers. In this context, the coffee shop market consists of retail stores, both specialist and nonspecialist (e.g., convenience stores), that sell freshly brewed coffee products. According to a report by iResearch, a leading market research firm in China, the country's coffee shop market was worth 87.6 billion yuan in 2021 and was expected to grow to 190 billion yuan by 2024.[7] To put this into perspective, China's retail book market was values at 98.7, 87.1 and 112.9 billion yuan in 2021, 2022 and 2024, respectively (see figure 5.4).[8] This disparity in market size helps explain why so many independent bookstores have turned to the coffee shop business as a strategy to navigate the challenges of the book retailing market.

What, then, makes independent bookstores competitive in China's already fiercely competitive coffee shop market? The answer lies in their two distinct strategic assets: their superior cultural appeal and ability to craft aesthetically unique spaces that deliver customers exceptional experiential value.

Generally speaking, establishing a coffee shop is a relatively low-cost venture for any retail business with suitable store space. In China, coffee machines and key ingredients are easy and inexpensive to source, thanks to the country's superb manufacturing and trade capabilities. While coffee preparation requires skills, baristas are relatively easy to hire or train in-house. Moreover,

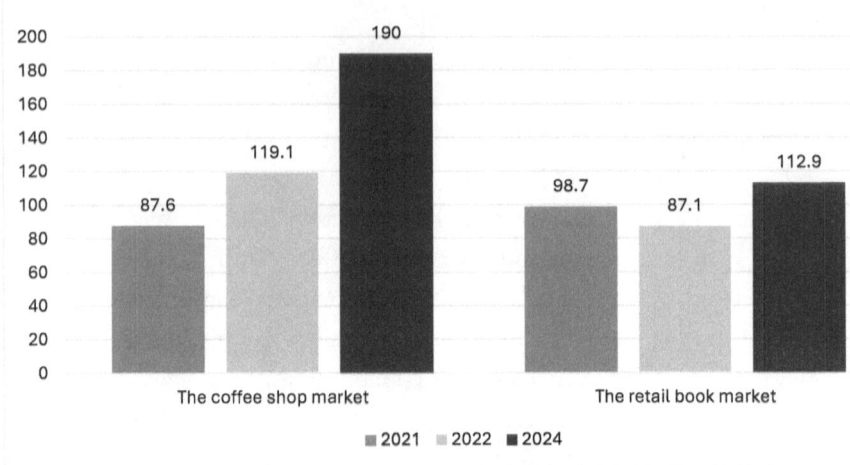

FIGURE 5.4 Actual and predicted market size of the coffee shop market and the retail book market in China (unit: billion yuan)

Sources: iResearch (2022), OpenBook (2023, 2025)

coffee shops do not require professional food preparation facilities, such as a full kitchen, as would be required for a restaurant. As a result, for independent bookstores already having physical spaces, establishing an in-store coffee shop is a relatively straightforward process requiring only modest financial and logistical investments, making it an appealing diversification option for them.

Meanwhile, according to a Deloitte report, a significant portion of China's coffee drinkers—67 percent and 51 percent, respectively—prioritize "comfortable Third Space offerings" and "unique design style" when choosing coffee shops.[9] The report concludes that coffee shops offering exceptional cultural experiences and values are more competitive in the Chinese market. It also reveals that consumers whose cultural needs are met tend to be less price-sensitive and more willing to pay premium prices for coffee products. These consumer preferences align perfectly with the strengths of independent bookstores—compared with specialist coffee shops like Starbucks, independent bookstores excel at creating and delivering exceptional cultural experiences and values. Their high-quality book collections exude an unparalleled cultural ambiance that enriches and elevates the coffee shop, whereas the various cultural events, which in many independent bookstores take place right in their attached coffee shops, further augment their cultural appeal, an appeal which is difficult for specialist coffee shops to effectively replicate.

In summary, the in-store coffee shop business stands out as the most popular diversification choice for independent bookstores for two main reasons. On the one hand, it is a highly financially rewarding and relatively straightforward business to establish and diversify into. On the other hand, with their unique ability to craft and deliver outstanding cultural experiences and values, independent bookstores are competitively placed to thrive in this lucrative business.

Selling Premium Nonbook Goods

While the practice of selling nonbook goods such as stationery, gifts, postcards, posters, mugs, tote bags, toys, board games, and so on is commonplace among bookshops worldwide, Chinese independent bookstores' approach to nonbook merchandising remains characteristic and worth examination. Two features are particularly interesting: the extensive range of products offered and their high prices.

My first impression of the nonbook goods sold in the independent bookstores I visited was their remarkable diversity. In all fairness, before my fieldwork, I had anticipated encountering some unconventional items beyond the usual stationery and gifts, in that my prefieldwork research had highlighted this trend. Even so, the sheer breadth and variety of non-book merchandise sold in some independent bookstores still exceeded my expectations. Among the unexpected items that caught my attention were wine, clothing, furniture, paintings, sculptures, china, perfume, jewelry, cutlery, cooking appliances, and even bicycles.

Figure 5.5 features a gift shop located within a large independent bookstore. According to this bookstore's manager, this gift shop carried more than three hundred different products, each with a unique stock keep unit (SKU), a code used by retailers for inventory identification and tracking. This particular gift shop was among the largest bookstore-run shops I visited during

FIGURE 5.5 A separate gift shop in an independent bookstore

Source: Author

my fieldwork, and most other independent bookstores maintained considerably smaller collections of nonbook goods. Even in some of the smallest bookstores, I encountered some carefully curated nonbook selections. In one such small bookstore in Beijing, which sold many delicate handmade artifacts, the owner told me that she sourced the items from local artists and art students and proudly remarked, "All my items are unique—you won't find them elsewhere." This dedication to curating appealing and distinctive nonbook offerings, however, was not unique to this particular store but was widely observed in many other independent bookstores I visited, suggesting a sector-wide emphasis on this diversification strategy.

What also struck me was the high price tag of many nonbook goods sold in these bookstores. Figure 5.6 shows a small

FIGURE 5.6 Small china set sold in an independent bookstore
Source: Author

set of china for sale for 2,800 yuan (approximately US$390) in an independent bookshop. Regardless of the item's intrinsic value or worth, this bookstore's decision to stock and sell such high-priced merchandise—especially considering the median new book price in 2019 was just 45 yuan—suggests that, when it comes to nonbook merchandising, independent bookstores clearly target the high-end market rather than the mass market. This approach thus highlights a distinctive feature of nonbook merchandising in independent bookstores. That is, instead of delivering value for money or utility, independent bookstores deliberately select products that convey an aura of exclusivity and fine taste to craft and market "sign value" to their customers. Sign value refers to a distinct form of commodity value pursued by status-conscious consumers to enhance their social standing through the consumption of goods or services that confer prestige.[10] By offering products with such value, independent bookstores actively seek to convert their rich cultural distinction into economic capital.

The independent booksellers I interviewed were candid about this motivation. Several explicitly stated that their primary goal for adopting nonbook merchandising was to boost profits. The owner of an independent bookstore chain with an extended nonbook product line said:

> We started selling nonbook products in 2008. A few years later, we founded our own stationery company to design our own-brand stationery to sell in all our stores. We put a lot of efforts into developing our nonbook line because we believe this is the only viable way forward for bookstores like us. Although we still focus on books, personally, I believe bookselling as a business has reached its growth limit—it will be very difficult to further grow

it. Last year, our nonbook sales grew by 100 percent, whereas our book sales increased by only 20 percent, which was mainly due to rising book prices. Currently, our nonbook sales account for about 20–30 percent of our overall revenue, lower than book sales' 50 percent. But in terms of profit, they are roughly equivalent.

Notably, this interviewee's bookstore is a very competitive and successful independent bookstore chain with multiple branches and sells mainly academic books, serious nonfiction, and high-quality literature. Its focus on these "scholarly books" is likely the reason why this interviewee considered diversifying into nonbook retailing "the only viable way forward." In contrast, nonindependent bookstores focused on commercial titles often can thrive purely by selling books without needing diversification.

A common sentiment among independent bookstores, therefore, is that maintaining a strong cultural commitment and a noncommercial ethos in bookselling is more important than profitability, even if this requires a highly commercial approach to the nonbook businesses they take up. Indeed, nonbook diversification tends to work more effectively in bookstores that maintain a clear demarcation between book-related and nonbook offerings, such as the above interviewee's bookstore. Notably, it seems that the less a bookstore appears driven by monetary considerations in bookselling—for instance, by prioritizing high-quality but low-market-appeal books—the more attractive it is to customers who are drawn to its nonbook offerings. This dynamic, I argue, underpins independent bookstores' seemingly paradoxical attitudes toward commercialism: a steadfast cultural commitment to bookselling and a pragmatic embrace of commercialism in nonbook diversifications.

SEEKING RENT REDUCTION BY GOING TO THE MALL

At the beginning of this chapter, I discussed how most independent bookstores struggle to make a profit from bookselling, citing one interviewee who attributed this challenge to the high rent these bookstores faced. This viewpoint was widely echoed by nearly all of the independent bookstore owners or managers I interviewed, who unanimously identified high rent as their greatest financial burden. Even those fortunate enough to own their premises also acknowledged the impact of high rent on the industry. As one owner candidly remarked: "I would have closed this store down a long time ago if I didn't own the property." High rent undermines independent bookstores through a "scissors effect": It creates a substantial gap between the high *expense* of rent and the modest *revenue* yielded by bookselling. In the previous section, we examined how many independent bookstores address this gap by diversifying their revenue streams. In this section, we explore how some seek to reduce their rent expenses.

Good Surprise

Roughly from the early 2010s, some popular independent bookstores in major cities like Beijing, Shanghai, and Hangzhou started to receive offers from commercial real estate developers—such as those developing and managing shopping malls, hotels, and office buildings—to relocate to or open new stores on their properties. These offers often came with significant incentives, such as reduced or fully waived rent and utility charges and reimbursements for relocation and store setup costs. Given that most offers came from large shopping malls, the following discussion will focus primarily on these entities and their motivations for courting independent bookstores.

The term *court* is appropriate here because these offers were typically initiated by shopping malls and often involved competition between rival malls to secure partnerships with their preferred bookstores. Such competition often took the form of escalating offers to outbid competitors or leveraging personal connections, such as mutual acquaintances, to persuade target bookstores to accept their proposals. Considering the economic disparity between shopping malls—multibillion-yuan corporate entities—and independent bookshops—small businesses often struggling to make ends meet—such competition may initially appear improbable. However, according to several interviewees who had received invitations from various shopping malls, the rivalry was not only real but could be very intense. For instance, the CEO of a highly popular independent bookstore chain in Beijing shared, "We receive several dozen such invitations every year. All of the major shopping malls in Beijing have approached us about opening stores with them, and we've also received offers from malls in Tianjin, Shanghai, and other cities." Similarly, the owner of a small yet renowned independent bookstore in Beijing said: "Many people have approached me through mutual friends, inviting me to open new stores in their real estate with zero rent. Some even offered to cover the new store's decoration costs. But I've declined them all because I don't want to expand."

Mixed Attitudes

For some independent bookstores—such as the first interviewee's company—the offers they received from shopping malls represented not only good news but also good surprises. The offers' generous terms could not only help alleviate these bookstores' financial burdens, especially high rent, but also enable them to grow by opening new stores. For example, the first interviewee's company, with the abundance of offers it received every year, managed to negotiate even more favorable terms with the malls and consequently opened several new stores within a few years in cities far from its hometown of Beijing—despite operating at a loss throughout this process.

In contrast, other independent bookstores—such as the second interviewee's company—showed little interest in these offers. These bookstores were already profitable and did not face immediate financial pressures that necessitated rent reductions. More important, however, their reluctance stemmed from their skepticism about the motivations behind the shopping malls' generosity and their concerns about potential pitfalls hidden in these tempting offers. When asked why they declined all the offers they received, the second interviewee said: "I was formerly a professional investor before taking early retirement to open this bookstore to pursue my passion for culture. As an ex-investor, I know all too well the motives behind this kind of so-called win-win collaboration. It's not a business partnership—it's more like an investment a shopping mall makes in a bookstore. Once you're in, you lose control of your business." This sentiment was echoed by another interviewee, who stressed that "maintaining independence" was more important than "saving on rent." This bookseller, the owner of a small yet profitable bookstore chain, revealed that they had turned down over eighty rent-waiving offers from various types of landlords, predominantly shopping malls.

Comparing these contrasting attitudes—embracing and rejecting—we can conclude that whereas those independent bookstores struggling to turn a profit, even with nonbook diversifications, are more receptive to rent-reduction offers from shopping malls, profitable independents tend to prioritize autonomy over more profits or expansion. This divergent attitude serves to highlight that, despite their shared cultural commitment, independent bookstores are driven by differing financial circumstances and imperatives and tend to act differently according to their specific economic conditions.

From this perspective, bookstores claiming that by collaborating with shopping malls, they aim to leverage the malls' economic resources to "pursue our own cultural goals," may appear to either underestimate the malls' high profit expectations or overestimate their own ability to navigate corporate rules and dynamics. As the second interviewee pointed out, like all lease agreements, these rent-reduction offers are fixed-term, usually lasting three to five years. During this period, the mall would regularly evaluate the bookstore's performance, primarily assessing its ability to attract customers to the mall and increase the mall's real estate value, especially rental rates. Regardless of the specific metrics used, shopping malls are unlikely to renew leases with bookstores unless there is clear evidence of financial gain resulting from these rent-free arrangements. Commenting on this, the abovementioned investor-turned-bookseller used his expert knowledge to elucidate: "Every investment requires returns. If you fail to deliver returns, you must either stay but pay the full rent or close the store and leave when the lease ends."

To triangulate my data, I sought insights from other interviewees regarding the inclusion of terms on returns in such rent-reduction offers and received varied responses. Most interviewees familiar with this matter concurred with the second interviewee, confirming that many of the offers they had received or heard about included clauses specifying the outcomes anticipated by the malls. These clauses often also specified the bookstore's obligations, such as hosting a certain number of events annually and meeting expected attendance levels.

A different account came from the first interviewee, who stated that they had never signed agreements containing explicit terms on expectations or returns. They said: "We receive so many offers every year and can choose the best ones we like. The offers we have accepted so far were mostly facilitated through mutual friends, so they're not that commercial in nature." Considering the popularity of this interviewee's bookstore, it likely possesses the negotiating power to exclude any restrictive, performance-related clauses from its agreements with the malls. However, for most other independent bookstores, entering such partnerships with shopping malls almost always involves varying degrees of commitment to delivering measurable commercial benefits of various kinds to the malls as part of their contracts.

Of course, for the vast majority of independent bookstores, such opportunities are out of reach—they might have heard stories of some famous bookstores securing zero-rent contracts, but they are seldom recipients of such offers. In other words, "seeking rent reduction by going to the mall" is a privileged game reserved for a few prominent independent bookstores and has little to do with the realities of most others. Discussing this, the owner of a small independent bookshop in Beijing commented: "It's only the famous ones that get those invitations, not bookstores like us. We can only rely on ourselves."

Shopping malls' preference for famous independent bookstores is straightforward and tied to their motivation for wanting to host a bookstore on their premises in the first place: to attract more customers through the bookstore's provision of diverse retail services—bookselling, events, nonbook merchandise, coffee shops, and more—while creating a distinctive cultural ambiance appealing to affluent consumers. These consumers are believed to be drawn to the cultural prestige associated with independent bookstores, hence making renowned independents more attractive to the malls than lesser-known stores.

Case Study: Sisyphe Bookstore

Although rent-reduction opportunities are limited to select independent bookstores, this strategy remains a critical lens for understanding the economic dynamics of independent bookselling, for it was a key driver behind the sector's remarkable growth during the 2010s. The impact of this practice is most evident in the success of one particular independent bookstore—Sisyphe Bookstore—whose success is widely attributed to its masterly leveraging of the power of the real estate sector to fuel its own expansion.

Sisyphe Bookstore is widely regarded as a pioneer independent bookstore in China. Its first shop was opened in 1993 in Zunyi, a historic but small town in Guizhou Province in southwestern China, by a group of university graduates. Like many other bookstores of the 1990s that are now considered the first generation of independent bookstores, Sisyphe thrived throughout the 1990s and the 2000s by focusing on selling high-quality intellectual and literary works. By 2005, it had grown into the largest privately owned bookstore chain in Guizhou Province. Despite its expansion, it retained its high cultural standards and, therefore, continued to be widely viewed as an independent bookstore.

A significant transformation began in 2008 with the appointment of a new president, Jin Weizhu. Prior to Jin's appointment, the company had struggled with declining sales and shrinking profits for several years due to a range of disruptive changes in the Chinese bookselling industry, such as the rise of online bookstores. On the brink of bankruptcy, Sisyphe turned to Jin, who resolved to overhaul the business completely. First, Jin and his team fully embraced diversification, making the in-store coffee shop and nonbook merchandising core components of every single Sisyphe branch. This configuration, formalized within the company as the "book-coffee-cultural product" trio, became a hallmark of the Sisyphe Bookstore brand (see figure 5.7). More important, Jin made the pivotal decision to partner with commercial real estate companies, primarily shopping malls, as part of a strategic expansion plan. By opening new stores in shopping malls, Sisyphe embarked on a path of rapid growth that, while not without controversy, has continued to shape the company's success to this day.

In 2008, the same year as Jin's inauguration, the Guizhou-born bookstore opened its first store outside of Guizhou Province in Chongqing, a major southwestern city. It was located in

FIGURE 5.7 A Sisyphe Bookstore

Source: Sisyphe Bookstore

Sanxia Square, a large shopping center in Shapingba District. By 2011, the company expanded into Chengdu, another bustling southwestern metropolis, where it opened several new stores, all in shopping malls under favorable rent-waiving agreements. Two years later, in 2013, Sisyphe ventured beyond the southwestern region for the first time, opening a store in Shenzhen, Guangdong Province, in southern China. This store was hosted by the Mixc, a landmark retail complex developed by China Resources, a leading real estate developer. China Resources went on to become a major partner of Sisyphe, facilitating its expansion into nearly all major Chinese cities over the following decade by hosting numerous Sisyphe stores in its extensive network of shopping malls nationwide. Through these strategic collaborations, Sisyphe Bookstore achieved a nationwide presence, with its rent-waiving-based strategy continuing to drive substantial growth.

In 2015, Sisyphe opened twenty new stores in Hangzhou, Xiamen, and Shanghai (the southeastern region). In 2017, it expanded into Beijing and Tianjin (the northern region), bringing its total number of stores to over one hundred. This remarkable growth continued into 2018 when the chain doubled its store count. By 2020, Sisyphe boasted more than three hundred stores in over eighty cities across China.[11] While Sisyphe's success can be attributed to a range of factors—not least its sophisticated, self-developed inventory management system and exceptional marketing capabilities, as highlighted by Jin on various occasions—its partnerships with shopping malls likely played the most important role. By securing rent-waiving agreements, Sisyphe effectively addressed the most pressing challenge for most independent bookstores—the high cost of rent. This strategy proved to be one of the most significant contributors to the company's rapid growth and sustained success.

Unsurprisingly, Sisyphe's expansion has sparked controversy within the independent bookselling community. Once regarded as an exemplary independent bookstore, Sisyphe's qualification has come under scrutiny following its significant expansion. The controversy centers around the chain's unapologetic embrace of commercial practices and perceived compromises in cultural standards. "Sisyphe has long ceased to be an independent bookstore. It now sells too many bestsellers!" remarked one interviewee when discussing the criteria for independent bookstores.

Fellow bookstores' criticisms, however, does not seem to have shaken the chain's determination to achieve financial viability through commercialization. In fact, the company now appears to be indifferent to the independent bookstore label altogether. For example, in the "About Us" section of its website, the company states, "From the initial ideal of being a humanities bookstore to developing as a chain, Sisyphe Bookstore has experienced a self-iteration from bookstore 1.0 to bookstore 2.0 and is now on its way to evolve into bookstore 3.0. Our vision is to become in the near future a culture service platform that synthesises cultural product retailing, cultural content creation, and cultural resources."[12] What this concise yet unequivocal statement conveys is the company's firm and unapologetic departure from its past as a highly regarded but financially struggling independent bookstore. Instead, it now positions itself as a commercially driven and financially successful bookstore that still aspires to contribute to the cultural life of its customers. This commitment is encapsulated in the company's mission to "play a role in the local spiritual life."

Despite its voluntary departure from its independent bookstore roots, Sisyphe Bookstore remains widely associated with the independent bookselling community by trade observers and customers alike. Consequently, its actions continue to influence this sector and its members. On the one hand, it can be argued that Sisyphe's success has inadvertently benefited other independent bookstores by popularizing the culture of independent bookselling among a broader audience—many of whom might not have otherwise been drawn to such establishments. By introducing and promoting the concepts of high-quality books, diverse culture-themed events, nonbook merchandise, and aesthetically pleasing store environments to a wider consumer base, Sisyphe Bookstore has arguably educated Chinese consumers on a new way of interacting with bookstores. This heightened consumer awareness of and demand for these offerings will benefit not only Sisyphe but also other independent bookstores, for an expanded market generally creates new opportunities for all participants, regardless of whether they approve of the methods driving this expansion.

On the other hand, certain members of the independent bookselling community may view the actions of bookstores like Sisyphe as detrimental to the ethos of independent bookselling. They argue that, in their pursuit of commercial success, these influential bookstores have, in some ways, rewritten the playbook on what it means to be an independent bookstore in China—independent of both political influence and commercial forces. While headlines announcing the launch of yet another independent bookstore in an upmarket shopping mall often have little relevance to the daily realities of the vast majority of independent bookstores, the extraordinary success of bookstores like Sisyphe can complicate matters for these small, struggling independents. These bookstores, despite their challenges, remain committed to preserving their independence from both political and commercial influences. Yet the commercial success of bookstores like Sisyphe risks redefining consumer expectations, creating an image of independent bookstores that deviates from the values and realities upheld by most members of the community. This shift can make the pursuit of true independence even more difficult for those dedicated to maintaining it.

Though not universally adopted by all independent bookstores, the practice of seeking rent reduction by going to the mall is essential for understanding the economic practices of independent bookstores. Most notably, it reveals these bookstores' mixed attitudes toward commercialism. A division clearly exists between those bookstores that fully embrace commercialization as a survival strategy and those opposing it, demonstrating the differing stances independent bookstores take when faced with economic pressures and challenges. While united by a shared cultural commitment, these bookstores are inevitably divided by their approaches to commercial dynamics integral to the bookselling business.

RECEIVING SUBSIDIES

The third and final solution employed by many independent bookstores to tackle the challenge of unprofitability in bookselling is securing subsidies from various sources. The term *subsidy* is used here to refer to a variety of financial resources or assistance that independent bookstores marshal to support their business operations. The three most prevalent types of subsidies are: (a) the bookstore owner's income from another job, (b) direct financial support from the bookstore's parent company, and (c) external investments. Among these, the first type is particularly relevant to small independent bookstores owned by individual proprietors. The second type pertains to bookstores owned by large corporations whose main businesses are outside of the book business. The third type of subsidy is relevant only to a small collection of independent bookstores seeking to expand and grow through capital operation.

"We All Have Other Jobs!"

"We all have other jobs!" was the response from an interviewee to my question of how she sustained herself financially when the small independent bookshop she co-owned with two friends—it was inconspicuously located in a ground-floor flat in an old residential community in Beijing—had never turned a profit since opening two years ago.

> AUTHOR: So what do you do?
> INTERVIEWEE: I am a freelance children's book illustrator, X runs a fashion boutique, and Y is a full-time designer. We are both owners and workers for our bookstore.
> AUTHOR: You all have other jobs, then why did you decide to open a bookshop?
> INTERVIEWEE: First of all, our jobs are all related to the book or the arts, so we wanted a space of our own to exhibit our designs and artworks and those of our friends. Secondly, Y and I are freelancers and needed a studio to work from. We were going to rent this place to use as our studio but then decided to make it both a studio and a bookshop open to everyone. For us, the "bookstore" is a very broad concept. We can sell books in it, but we can also display our works, host small exhibitions, meet with friends, and so on. So we might not be the typical kind of bookstores you're researching about.

This co-owner correctly pointed out that her bookstore differed from the typical bookstore—a retail establishment set up to generate profits for its proprietor by selling books—due to the blurred boundaries between its retail function and its broad social function for its three co-owners. However, the assumption that this bookshop was unique among the independent bookstores I was studying was mistaken. In fact, it was representative of a collection of independent bookstores I came across whose owners did not establish them for making financial gains through bookselling. Rather, these owners all planned to use their bookstores primarily as platforms for wider social and cultural engagements beyond book retailing. In most of these cases, the owners had other incomes to sustain themselves financially so their livelihoods were not dependent on their bookstores' profitability. Consequently, what drove them to establish their stores was not economic considerations but a distinct desire to create venues for broader social and cultural practices and participation.

Among such bookstore owners I interviewed included two civil servants, a university lecturer, an investment bank manager, a couple working in the advertising sector, several freelance designers, a bar owner, and a couple who owned a stationery company. These individuals typically divided their time between their primary jobs—which provided them with stable incomes—and managing their bookstores. They thus differed from full-time bookstore owners whose livelihoods depended on their bookstores' profitability. Besides these part-time booksellers, there were three interviewees who were working full-time at their bookstores, but they—an ex-lawyer, ex-director of a real estate company, and ex-investor—were all so financially secure thanks to their previous careers that they could devote more time and resources to their bookstores than those part-time booksellers, who at least must work their main jobs for stable incomes.

Therefore, to say that an independent bookstore is subsidized by its owner does not necessarily mean that the owner uses their other income to cover the bookstore's expenses, such as rent. While such a scenario does exist, in most cases, "receiving subsidies from the owner" does not imply that the bookstore is subsidized in monetary terms by its proprietor but simply describes how the owner derives their main income from other sources and therefore maintains a low profit expectation for the bookstore, content with a modest profit or simply breaking even.

One interviewee, who held a full-time job in advertising, explained to me his rationale for opening a bookstore with his wife: "We didn't expect to make a lot of money from running this bookstore. We only hoped that it could break even so that we wouldn't have to invest too much in it but could still have the joy of owning a bookstore." To his delight, his store, which consistently stocked around seven thousand titles, included an attached coffee shop, and regularly hosted well-attended events, had been profit-making since opening.

Of course, there are instances where a bookstore demands monetary subsidies. For example, as highlighted to me by the couple who owned and ran a successful stationery company, they regularly had to use the stationery company's profits to pay for the bookstore's rent and other expenses. Similarly, another interviewee expressed his frustration with the large amount of freelance design work he had to undertake to support his family and the bookstore's operations in the face of rising rent and shrinking sales.

In summary, a considerable number of independent bookstores opened over the last two decades were founded by affluent individuals who did not rely on these businesses to make a living but instead used their bookstores as platforms for pursuing their personal passions for books, culture, the arts, and related interests. These individuals tended to identify themselves as bibliophiles and often cited a long-held aspiration to "fulfill the dream of being a bookseller" as a key motivation for opening their bookstores. That is, what drove these individuals to enter bookselling at a challenging time for brick-and-mortar retailers was the idea of immersing themselves in the world of books and culture while being able to ignore the financial implications of this endeavor to some extent, thanks to their economic privilege. While they might be a minority on the whole, a good number of independent bookstores opened in the last two decades were established by individuals like them.

Receiving Subsidies from Parent Companies and External Investors

Parallel to the establishment of independent bookstores by affluent, passion-driven individuals was the founding of independent bookstores by large, nonbook corporations. I refer to these companies as nonbook to highlight their externality to the book industry prior to their venture into independent bookselling. Not all bookstores established by such nonbook corporations identified themselves as independent bookstores. Nevertheless, some did enthusiastically embrace this label, basing their claim to independence on their parent companies' nonstate ownership.

NONBOOK CORPORATIONS

As previously discussed, from the early 2010s, independent bookselling began to attract the attention of some large, nonbook corporations who saw value in this business. These corporations came from diverse sectors, ranging from real estate, manufacturing, banking, export trading, fashion, and tourism.

During my fieldwork, I interviewed three bookstore managers working at bookstores founded by such nonbook corporations. At the time, all three bookstores were fully financed by their parent companies due to unprofitability.

According to these managers and others, nonbook corporations invested in independent bookstores because they believed the bookstores could help enhance their brand image and reputation. Rather than seeking direct or substantial financial returns from these investments, the corporations sought added value such as increased brand recognition and elevated brand prestige. They anticipated that owning their own-brand independent bookstores would lend a desired cultural distinction to their brand identity. In this sense, establishing independent bookstores functions similarly to marketing techniques like advertising and sponsorship. One interviewee explained:

> With the market void created by the closure of many small bookstores in the past decade, more and more large companies will enter this field. These companies have the capital and see value in the cultural prestige of bookstores. . . . XX Bank has recently opened a bookstore in Shanghai. Investing a few million yuan a year in a bookstore is trivial for a multibillion-yuan giant like it. Similarly, the owner of [an independent bookstore chain] also owns a real estate company. He set up the bookstores to drive up popularity and overall brand value of his shopping malls. This will, in turn, attract more businesses to lease space in his malls, yielding much more profits than what's been invested in the bookstore. So he doesn't need the bookstores to make money directly, as the money invested in them can be earned back through other channels.

A second reason identified by many interviewees for nonbook corporations' investment in independent bookselling was their plan to use the bookstore business as a stepping stone for venturing into the broader cultural and creative industries. Facing growth pressures in their own sectors, these corporations recognized the potential of the cultural and creative industries. However, rather than fully diving into this new and unfamiliar territory, they chose to test the waters by investing in the relatively low-cost and low-risk business of book retailing.

This rationale was highlighted to me by one interviewee, who was the managing director of an independent bookstore chain established by a manufacturing company.[13] He stated: "This bookstore is part of our parent company's expansion into the cultural industry. Their plans include establishing a parenting education firm, so we stock many children's books and host many family-themed events to prepare for that." Like this bookstore's parent company, many other nonbook corporations regard independent bookselling—or bookselling generally—as a low-risk, high-gain gateway to diversifying into industries with high growth potentials, such as the cultural and creative industries. This investment is considered low-risk, high-gain because it allows the companies to explore new growth opportunities while simultaneously mitigating the risks associated with delving into unfamiliar domains.

Not everyone, however, agreed that independent bookselling was low-risk, particularly the traditional type of independent booksellers. This perception was relative, shaped by the nonbook corporations' experiences in their own, often more volatile sectors, which led them to believe that, with proper risk management, independent bookselling could be a profitable—however modest—investment. One interviewee elaborated:

> The shifting economic landscape in recent years has affected many business people's perceptions of acceptable profit margins.

In the past, those in sectors like foreign trade and investment wouldn't even consider investing in businesses with profit margins below 12 percent. But with the economic downturns in their own industries, bookselling's 6–8 percent margin is now acceptable to them. A 6–8 percent net margin is at least better than bank interest rates, meaning investing in bookstores can at least be more profitable than keeping the money in the bank.

An important factor underlying this interviewee's positive assessment of independent bookstores' profit potential (a 6–8 percent net margin) is a favorable tax policy introduced in 2013. This policy exempts all book wholesalers and retailers, whether state-owned or privately owned, from the value added tax (VAT). Prior to this policy, book wholesalers and retailers were subject to a 17 percent VAT. Several interviewees identified this tax exemption as a major catalyst for nonbook corporations' entry into book retailing. One bookstore owner remarked: "The 17 percent VAT rate was quite high. Removing it means that a bookstore can save 1.7 million yuan on the sale of every 10 million yuan worth of books. This is a substantial amount."

Meanwhile, around the same time as the introduction of the tax exemption policy by the central government, many local governments across China launched bookstore subsidy schemes aimed at supporting physical bookstores. The specific terms of these schemes—such as subsidy amounts—varied, but the core idea behind them was identical: Any physical bookstore, whether state or privately owned, could apply for a one-off subsidy used for supporting their core, book-related operations, such as refurbishing stores, paying rent, and opening new branches.

Like the tax exemption policy, many of these subsidy schemes have since been extended and renewed, continuing to benefit physical bookstores, including the independents. In a recent conversation with an independent bookstore owner I initially interviewed in 2014, I learned that his bookstore was awarded a 100,000 yuan subsidy by its local government in 2022. He used the grant to completely refurbish the store, including removing the in-store coffee shop and reallocating the space to accommodate more books, which he was able to purchase with this grant.

"The coffee shop became largely redundant during the COVID-19 pandemic, whereas in the meantime we experienced a surge in online book sales for many people had to stay indoors or worked from home," this owner explained to me during a WeChat conversation in early 2023. "I used this grant to expand my inventory and invested in some much-needed live-streaming equipment for our online WeChat store." This account highlights the appeal of government subsidies for independent bookstores, suggesting that such financial incentives could have played a role in catalyzing nonbook corporations' entry into (independent) bookselling.

VENTURE CAPITAL

Venture capitalists (VCs) investing in independent bookstores were drawn to this sector by the same incentives discussed above, except for wanting prestige and brand recognition. Like the nonbook corporations, these investors also recognized the growth potentials of independent bookstores, especially those that had morphed into multifunctional cultural spaces. The favorable tax policy and government subsidies also registered in their drive to invest in independent bookstores.

That said, it is important to note that VC-backed independent bookstores represented a very small minority. Of all the independent bookstores I studied, only one had received VC investment. Notably, this bookstore had already established itself as a leading independent bookstore before the investment, and it was its advantageous industry position that made this investment possible, not vice versa. Using this investment, this bookstore opened several new branches across different cities. However, the bulk of the funding was not used for expanding the bookselling business but went toward developing a range of media and cultural products and services, including a social media app, a digital publishing program, and a television show.[14] Despite diversifying into these nonbook-related areas, it retained its reputation as a leading and exemplary independent bookstore.

Unfortunately, I was unable to persuade the bookstore's managing director, whom I interviewed in 2014, to provide an update on its development since the investment. Publicly available information, including media reports, the company's website, and its social media content, suggests that the company likely failed to achieve the level of growth the investor would have anticipated. For instance, the social media app it was diligently developing in 2014 with the aim of making it the Chinese version of Reddit is no longer available on any of the mainstream app stores. Moreover, in 2020, the bookstore launched a mass crowdfunding campaign to raise funds. Additionally, according to CVSource, a leading VC database, the company did not receive any further VC investment after its initial angel funding round.[15] In the world of venture capital, the lack of subsequent funding rounds typically suggests underperformance during the current round and a low valuation in the capital market. It also usually indicates a loss for the initial investors, as VCs typically profit—or exit—by selling their shares in a company to investors of later funding rounds. The absence of follow-up investments is commonly a sign of poor performance by the investee company. Collectively, this information suggests that this bookstore not only failed to achieve profitability (which is common for high-valuation start-ups) but also failed to deliver returns for its initial investor due to underperformance and a low valuation.

As a juxtaposition to this bookstore, we can consider Sisyphe Bookstore, which we discussed in the previous section. As mentioned, Sisyphe's remarkable expansion over the past decade has been attributed to several factors, including a significant external investment reportedly received from a VC firm. It is widely speculated that this investment allowed the company to open hundreds of new stores within a few years. Although I was unable to verify this information directly with the company, publicly available data offers some useful insights. For example, CVSource's record shows that Sisyphe received an angel investment in 2016, listed as "several million yuan."[16] While this figure is lower than what some journalists have reported and significantly lower than the US$10 million investment received by the previous bookstore, it still suggests that Sisyphe's rapid growth during the 2010s likely benefited from some sort of external financial backing. Although Sisyphe's expansion has led many other independent bookstores to disqualify it as an independent, its trajectory remains a telling example of how some independent bookstores have striven to overcome their economic challenges by embracing commercial practices despite the widely perceived tensions between such practices and the cultural aura commonly associated with these establishments.

CONCLUSION

This book has examined the rise, development, and evolving dynamics of independent bookstores in China, situating them within the broader cultural, economic, and political landscape of the Chinese book industry. It demonstrates that independent bookstores, far from being passive participants in the book market, actively negotiate their dual roles as cultural institutions and commercial enterprises. They achieve this by employing three culturally adapted strategies: political framing, moral positioning, and cultural distinguishing, which allow them to navigate the complex intersections between culture, commerce, and politics in the Chinese book industry.

One of this book's key arguments is that independent bookstores in China do not conform to the Western concept of "independent bookstores" as locally owned and nonchain enterprises. Instead, their independence is defined by a deep commitment to cultural values and cultural autonomy and a self-positioning that differentiates them both from the state-owned Xinhua Bookstore and commercially driven privately owned bookstores. This distinction is crucial, as it reflects a broader trend in China's cultural production field—where actors seek to carve out a space that balances economic survival with cultural autonomy.

Furthermore, this book has contributed to the understanding of the Chinese book industry by contextualizing the emergence and development of independent bookstores within the broader transformations in the book publishing, distribution, and retailing sectors. The structural and institutional forces shaping the book trade—including the interactions between state-owned publishing houses and privately owned book publishing companies, the dominance of Xinhua Bookstore in bookselling, and the disruptive impact of online platforms—are all shown to be critical for understanding the rise, strategies, and survival mechanisms of independent bookstores.

Another significant contribution of this book is its challenge to the dominant resistance narrative in English language literature on Chinese cultural production. Rather than portraying independent bookstores as politically oppositional entities, I argue that their strategies are primarily driven by cultural and economic motives. That is, their primary motivations are cultural and economic rather than political. Unlike some other nonstate-owned, independent media or cultural organizations in China, which may position themselves in opposition to the state, independent bookstores engage in political framing as a strategy to carve out their unique space in the highly competitive book retailing sector. Their engagement with political discourse in this process serves mainly as a means of differentiation rather than confrontation or resistance. This perspective nuances the understanding of nonstate cultural production in China, demonstrating that agency is exercised through strategic positioning rather than direct confrontation.

Another critical finding of this book is the role of moral positioning in the identity construction and strategy of independent bookstores. These bookstores often differentiate themselves from mainstream commercial enterprises by projecting an image of cultural and moral superiority. This involves carefully curating their book selections, fostering intellectual discussions, and hosting events that align with their brand identity. By doing so, they attract a customer base that values not only the content of their books but also the ethos of the bookstore itself.

The strategy of cultural distinguishing further solidifies the identity of independent bookstores as distinct from both state-run and commercial bookstores. This is achieved through unique store aesthetics, branding, and in-store experiences designed to appeal to customers seeking intellectual engagement and cultural differentiation. As such, beyond their commercial activities, independent bookstores also significantly contribute to the cultural landscape of contemporary China by serving as important spaces for literary discussion, intellectual exchange, and cultural engagement. Their ability to survive and even thrive in a highly competitive environment, therefore, is creditable not only to these organizations' abilities to innovate and adapt but also to the marketplace's demand for alternative cultural spaces.

In addition, this book has highlighted the significance of historical precedents in shaping the current independent bookselling practices. The proliferation of scholarly bookstores in the 1990s provided a foundation for the independent bookstore movement, demonstrating a longstanding tradition of intellectual and literary engagement outside state-owned book publishing and retailing spaces. By tracing this historical trajectory, the book has provided a richer understanding of the cultural and intellectual roots of independent bookselling in China.

Lastly, the findings of this book also have broader implications beyond the Chinese context. By introducing the concept of culturally adapted strategies, this study offers a framework that can be applied to analyze cultural enterprises operating under similar economic and political settings. The nuanced approach taken here—acknowledging the coevolution of cultural, economic, and political logics—provides a valuable lens for future research on how independent cultural businesses globally navigate challenges and opportunities across different sociopolitical landscapes. The challenges faced by independent bookstores are not unique to China but are part of a broader global trend where independent cultural enterprises struggle to maintain autonomy in the face of market and political pressures. The Chinese case presented in this book thus offers an instructive example of how such enterprises can navigate these pressures through strategic positioning and adaptive practices. By balancing cultural and economic imperatives, independent bookstores in China exemplify a model of resilience that is relevant to cultural businesses worldwide.

In conclusion, independent bookstores in China represent a distinctive phenomenon within the country's evolving book culture. Their ability to simultaneously embrace cultural aspirations and economic imperatives highlights the adaptability and resilience of nonstate-owned cultural enterprises in contemporary China. By illuminating their strategies, challenges, and contributions, this book has provided a comprehensive and critical account of an important yet understudied sector of the Chinese cultural economy. Future research could build upon these insights by examining how independent bookstores continue to evolve in response to shifting market conditions, policy changes, and technological disruptions in the years to come.

Indeed, the engagement of independent bookstores with digital technology has become a critical dimension of their development in recent years. While initially positioned in opposition to the rise of online book retailing, many independent bookstores have since embraced e-commerce, social media marketing, livestreaming, and digital community-building strategies into their operations. Online platforms such as WeChat, Douyin, and Xiaohongshu (RedNote) have become essential tools for booksellers to reach wider audiences, organize virtual events, and cultivate brand loyalty. These digital adaptations highlight the capacity of independent bookstores to leverage new technologies while preserving their core cultural identities. As digital transformations continue to reshape the book industry and wider cultural and creative industries in China, independent bookstores must further innovate to meet changing consumer demands and adapt to new technological challenges and opportunities.

Since my fieldwork, the world of independent bookstores has continued to evolve, with the COVID-19 pandemic exerting a particularly profound impact. Many struggling independent bookstores were forced to fold due to sharply declining sales, while others sought innovative ways to survive. Among the most significant developments has been the rapid proliferation of live-streaming e-commerce in China since the mid-2010s, which has opened up unexpected opportunities for some independent bookstores. Determined not to succumb, several of the bookstores I studied have turned to live-streaming to reach readers afield, navigating new challenges while also rediscovering the joy of connecting with readers across the country through sharing books and culture. This revolutionary technology has enabled these bookstores to discover new territories that were previously unknown or simply out of reach to them.

Rediscovering the joy of simply being a bookstore that focuses on selling good books—a joy that has been somewhat lost amid the pressures of diversification in the past decade—some independent bookstores have also begun to move away from diversification and recenter bookselling as their core business. In the summer of 2024, for example, I visited one such independent bookstore that had managed to achieve six-digit monthly sales figures by selling books only. This bookshop presents a stark contrast with the struggling bookstore I cited at the beginning of chapter 5, which struggled to generate 2,220 yuan in daily book sales. Opened in 2017 and located in the capital of an eastern province, the owner of this single-store operation attributes his business's success to a simple principle: "Selling the best books at the lowest possible prices." Eschewing the usual add-ons of independent bookstores—such as fancy coffee shops, profitable nonbook merchandise, or traffic-attracting events—this "conventional" bookstore, or "1.0-version bookstore," as the owner describes it, seems to have discovered the secret to being a profitable independent bookstore in the age of multifunctional bookstore-cultural spaces—curating the best books and leveraging bulk purchasing to secure the most favorable discount terms.

Of course, capitalizing on digital technologies remains crucial. The owner of this bookstore, for example, manages seven mobile phones to run the seven WeChat accounts that he uses to maintain close connections with and market books to his more than thirty thousand WeChat "friends"—a loyal customer base that constitutes the majority of his day-to-day sales. This case highlights the surprising yet vital power of digital engagement in sustaining a successful, albeit small-scale, bookselling business in today's China. Digital technology is transforming businesses of all sizes by redefining both the methods and the boundaries of doing business beyond mere e-commerce and digitalization.

The evolution of independent bookstores in recent years has, therefore, been both revealing and fascinating. On the one hand, some bookstores are scaling back diversification and reverting to their core mission of selling books. On the other hand, many continue to expand into multifunctional cultural hubs where books play a secondary role. While it is impossible to predict which path will prove more sustainable for the majority of independent bookstores, one thing remains clear and unchanged about these establishments—their shared ethos of always embracing difference, experimenting with novel methods, and exploring unknown territories to navigate ever-shifting market environments.

GLOSSARY

Chinese term	Term in Pinyin	English translation
独立书店	duli shudian	independent bookstore
出版社	chuban she	publishing house
图书公司	tushu gongsi	book company
新闻出版署	xinwen chuban shu	National Press and Publication Administration (NPPA)
中央级出版社	zhongyang ji chuban she	central-level publishing house
地方级出版社	difang ji chuban she	regional-level publishing house
主办单位	zhuban danwei	applicant entity
主管机关	zhuguan jiguan	supervising organ
出版管理条例	chuban guanli tiaoli	Regulations on Publication Administration
出版物市场管理规定	Chubanwu shichang guanli guiding	Provisions on the Administration of the Publication Market
省	sheng	province
自治区	zizhi qu	autonomous region
直辖市	zhixia shi	municipalities
合作出版	hezuo chuban	collaborative publishing
书号买卖	shuhao maimai	book number sale
一书一号	yishu yihao	one book one number
三审制	sanshen zhi	three-step examination

(continued)

Chinese term	Term in Pinyin	English translation
责任编辑	zeren bianji	responsible editor
主渠道	zhu qudao	main channel
二渠道	er qudao	secondary channel
新华书店	xinhua shudian	Xinhua Bookstore
外文书店	waiwen shudian	Foreign Language Bookstore
省店	shengdian	provincial head store
市店	shidian	municipal head store
中盘商	zhongpan shang	middle dealer
事业单位	shiye danwei	public service organisation

NOTES

INTRODUCTION

1. Giles Clark and Angus Phillips, *Inside Book Publishing*, 6th ed. (Routledge, 2019); Robert Baensch, *The Publishing Industry in China* (Routledge, 2017); Guangwei Xin, *Publishing in China: An Essential Guide*, 2nd ed. (Cengage Learning, 2010).
2. Laura J. Miller, *Reluctant Capitalists: Bookselling and the Culture of Consumption* (University of Chicago Press, 2006); John B. Thompson, *Merchants of Culture: The Publishing Business in the Twenty-First Century* (Polity, 2010).
3. Thompson, *Merchants of Culture*, 25.
4. Thorstein Veblen, *The Theory of the Leisure Class* (Houghton Mifflin, 1899 [1973]).
5. See, for example, Eric Kit-wai Ma, "Rethinking Media Studies: The Case of China," in *De-Westernizing Media Studies*, ed. James Curran and Myung-Jin Park (Routledge, 2005), 17–28; Chin-Chuan Lee, "Rethinking Political Economy: Implications for Media and Democracy in Greater China," *Javnost—the Public* 8, no. 4 (2001): 81–102; Yuezhi Zhao, *Communication in China: Political Economy, Power, and Conflict* (Rowman & Littlefield, 2008).
6. See, for example, Jacques DeLisle, Avery Goldstein, and Guobin Yang, eds., *The Internet, Social Media, and a Changing China* (University of Pennsylvania Press, 2016); Maria Repnikova, *Media Politics in China: Improvising Power Under Authoritarianism* (Cambridge University Press, 2017).

7. Alan Bryman, *Social Research Methods*, 5th ed. (Oxford University Press, 2012), 32–33.
8. Bryman, *Social Research Methods*, 27.
9. Pierre Bourdieu, *The Field of Cultural Production: Essays on Art and Literature* (Polity, 1993).
10. Dave Elder-Vass, *The Reality of Social Construction* (Cambridge University Press, 2012).

1. BOOK PUBLISHING AND RETAILING IN CHINA

1. This book discusses the book publishing and retailing industries in the mainland area of the People's Republic of China. The discussion does not apply to the book publishing and retailing industries in other Chinese territories including Hong Kong, Macao, and Taiwan.
2. The NPPA is the highest central government department overseeing the press and publication sectors. A China Standard Book Number consists of an International Standard Book Number (ISBN) and a unique book classification number.
3. Guangwei Xin, *Publishing in China: An Essential Guide*, 2nd ed. (Cengage Learning, 2010), 5.
4. Giles Clark and Angus Phillips, *Inside Book Publishing*, 6th ed. (Routledge, 2019).
5. Xin, *Publishing in China*, 43.
6. Qidong Yun, "State Versus Market: A Perspective on China's Publishing Industry," *Logos* 24, no. 1 (2013): 19–29, https://doi.org/10.1163/1878-4712-11112009.
7. The three-step examination is a quality-control measure in place in the Chinese book publishing industry. Before a book manuscript can be sent out for production, it must be examined and approved by three editors to ensure it meets all relevant quality standards. The first examination is usually conducted by the book's commissioning editor, the editor who has taken care of the project up to this point. The first examination is to ensure that the manuscript is free of editorial errors as well as common knowledge, legal, political, and other errors. The manuscript is then sent for second examination by a senior editor in the house before

a final examination and approval by the editor-in-chief, head of house, or their appointed delegate.
8. John B. Thompson, *Merchants of Culture: The Publishing Business in the Twenty-First Century* (Polity, 2010).
9. NPPA, *2019 Nian Quanguo Xinwen Chubanye Jiben Qingkuang* (*National Press and Publishing Report 2019*) (NPPA, 2020).
10. Qingguo Sun, "Economics of the Chinese Book Market," *Publishing Research Quarterly* 18, no. 3 (2003): 54–63.
11. Deyan Yang, "The Reform of the Book Distribution Industry and the Development of Non-State-Owned Bookstores in China," *Publishing Research Quarterly* 18, no. 2 (2002): 50–55.
12. NPPA, *1999 Nian Quanguo Xinwen Chubanye Jiben Qingkuang* (*National Press and Publishing Report 1999*) (NPPA, 2000); Yang, "The Reform of the Book Distribution Industry."
13. For clarity, in this book I use the term "academic book" to refer to academic monographs and textbooks written by and for academic researchers and the term "scholarly book" to refer to the kind of high-quality serious intellectual books sold by scholarly bookstores in the 1990s and by independent bookstores today.
14. Min Yu et al., "Zhongguo Minying Shuye Fazhan Yanjiu Baogao," *Chuban Faxing Yanjiu* [Publishing research], 11 (2003): 5–21.
15. OpenBook, *Annual Report on the Chinese Book Retailing Market (2016)* (OpenBook, 2017).
16. Duncan Clark, *Alibaba: The House That Jack Ma Built* (Ecco, 2016).
17. Wenbo Kuang, "Feichang Shiqi De Wangmin Xingwei Tezheng," *Guoji Xinwenjie* [Journal of international communication], no. 5 (2003): 24–27.
18. Thompson, *Merchants of Culture*.
19. Ting Wen, "Dangdang Wang Er Jidu Jingli 2880 Wan, Chuang Lishi Xingao," *Shanghai Securities News*, August 15, 2014, https://paper.cnstock.com/html/2014-08/15/content_434834.htm.
20. Pan Zhang, "Tushu Wangshou Shichang: Dangdang, Jingdong, Amazon Sanfen Tianxia De Xi Yu You," *Zhongguo Chuban Chuanmei Shangbao* [China publishing & media journal], October 30, 2014, 14.
21. Analysys, *2016 Nian Diyi Jidu Zhongguo B2C Shichang Tushu Chubanwu Pinlei Shichang Fen'e* (Analysys, 2016), https://www.analysys.cn/article/detail/1000089.

22. Michael A. Cusumano, Annabelle Gawer, and David B. Yoffie, *The Business of Platforms: Strategy in the Age of Digital Competition, Innovation, and Power* (Harper Business, 2019).
23. CBNData, *2021 Tushu Xiaofei Bannian Baogao* (CBNData, 2021).
24. OpenBook, *Annual Report on the Chinese Book Retailing Market (2019)* (OpenBook, 2020).
25. OpenBook, *Annual Report on the Chinese Book Retailing Market (2019)*.
26. Alibaba, "Alibaba Jituan Gongbu 2021 Nian Sanyuefen Jidu Ji 2021 Cainian Yeji," https://ali-home.alibaba.com/document-1491839814327074816, accessed June 13, 2025.
27. "Tushu Fenxiao Xin Shengtai: Geju Yu Qushi," *China Publishing Today*, June 8, 2016, https://www.jxxhsd.com/read_txt.asp?type=12&id=3452.

2. SEARCHING FOR AN INDEPENDENT IDENTITY

1. Laura J. Miller, *Reluctant Capitalists: Bookselling and the Culture of Consumption* (University of Chicago Press, 2006), 164–65.
2. Miller, *Reluctant Capitalists*, 165.
3. Miller, *Reluctant Capitalists*, 164–65.
4. "Capital operation" is a term used in China to describe the strategic use of various financial tools, such as capital investments, to enable a company to achieve business goals that cannot be attained with its existing assets.
5. Miller, *Reluctant Capitalists*.
6. Xiaosong Zhang and Jichai Zhu, "Xi Jinping tan Wenchuang Chanye: Shouzheng Chuangxin, Jianchi Zhengque Daoxiang," *Xinhua Shidian*, September 18, 2020, http://politics.people.com.cn/n1/2020/0918/c1024-31866673.html.
7. Pierre Bourdieu, *The Field of Cultural Production: Essays on Art and Literature* (Polity, 1993).
8. Cambridge English Dictionary, "Individuality," https://dictionary.cambridge.org/dictionary/english/individuality, accessed May 16, 2022.
9. Miller, *Reluctant Capitalists*, 165.
10. Yuanchong Xu, "Congxin Suoyu Erbu Yueju—Tan Shici Fanyi Yu Zhongguo Wenhua Meng," *Guangming Daily*, April 28, 2015, https://epaper.gmw.cn/gmrb/html/2015-04/28/nw.D110000gmrb_20150428_1-11.htm.

11. Niklas Luhmann, *The Making of Meaning: From the Individual to Social Order: Selections from Niklas Luhmann's Works on Semantics and Social Structure*, ed. Christian Morgner, trans. Margaret Hiley, Christian Morgner, and Michael King (Oxford University Press, 2022).
12. Zheng Liu, "Between Business and Morality: Cultural Politics of Independent Bookshops in China," *Journal of Cultural Economy* 13, no. 4 (2020): 461–74.

3. CULTURALLY ADAPTED STRATEGIES: THE CONCEPT

1. NPPA, *2019 Nian Quanguo Xinwen Chubanye Jiben Qingkuang* (*National Press and Publishing Report 2019*) (NPPA, 2020).
2. Yang Yu, "Sanfen Zhiyi Tushu Zhixiao, Tamen Douqu Na'er Le?" [One-third of published books are left unsold. Where have they gone to?], *Chuban Ren* [China Publishers] 12 (2017): 32–36.
3. Laura J. Miller, *Reluctant Capitalists: Bookselling and the Culture of Consumption* (University of Chicago Press, 2006).
4. Heng Zhao, *Quan Xue Shi*, year unknown. Translated by the author.
5. Alexander Des Forges, "Burning with Reverence: The Economics and Aesthetics of Words in Qing (1644–1911) China," *PMLA/Publications of the Modern Language Association of America* 121, no. 1 (2006): 141.
6. Des Forges, "Burning with Reverence," 141.
7. Des Forges, "Burning with Reverence," 142.
8. Des Forges, "Burning with Reverence," 143–44.
9. Lu Xun, "Men Wai Wen Tan," *Shen Bao* (August 24–September 10, 1934).
10. Vladimir I. Lenin, *The State and Revolution* (International Publishers, 1968).
11. Pierre Bourdieu, "The Forms of Capital," *Cultural Theory: An Anthology* 1 (2011): 81–93.
12. Pierre Bourdieu, *The Field of Cultural Production: Essays on Art and Literature* (Polity, 1993).
13. OpenBook, *Annual Report on the Chinese Book Retailing Market (2019)* (OpenBook, 2020).
14. Pierre Bourdieu, "Vive ls Crise! For Heterodoxy in Social Science," *Theory and Society* 17 (1988): 783.

15. Thorstein Veblen, *The Theory of the Leisure Class* (Houghton Mifflin, 1899 [1973]).
16. Veblen, *The Theory of the Leisure Class*, 60.
17. Diana Farrell et al., *From 'Made in China' to 'Sold in China': The Rise of the Chinese Urban Consumer* (McKinsey, 2006); Dominic Barton, Yougang Chen, and Amy Jin, *Mapping China's Middle Class* (McKinsey, 2013); Homi Kharas and Meagan Dooley, *China's Influence on the Global Middle Class* (Brookings Institution, 2020); Aimee Kim, Lan Luan, and Daniel Zipser, *The Chinese Luxury Consumer* (McKinsey, 2019); Jennifer S. Maguire and Hu Dan, "Not a Simple Coffee Shop: Local, Global and Glocal Dimensions of the Consumption of Starbucks in China," *Social Identities* 19, no. 5 (2013): 670–84.
18. Elisabeth Croll, *China's New Consumers: Social Development and Domestic Demand* (Routledge, 2006).
19. Barton, Chen, and Jin, *Mapping China's Middle Class*.
20. Jinyuan Investment Group and Hurun Report, *2018 Zhongguo Xinzhongchan Quanceng Baipishu (Hurun 2018 China New Middle Class Report)*, https://res.hurun.cn/file/20190910/20190910143413876288.pdf, accessed June 13, 2025.
21. Croll, *China's New Consumers*.

4. IMPLEMENTING CULTURALLY ADAPTED STRATEGIES

1. NPPA, *2019 Nian Quanguo Xinwen Chubanye Jiben Qingkuang (National Press and Publishing Report 2019)* (NPPA, 2020).
2. John B. Thompson, *Merchants of Culture: The Publishing Business in the Twenty-First Century* (Polity, 2010), 262.
3. Laura J. Miller, *Reluctant Capitalists: Bookselling and the Culture of Consumption* (University of Chicago Press, 2006), 69.
4. John B. Thompson, *Books in the Digital Age: The Transformation of Academic and Higher Education Publishing in Britain and the United States* (Polity, 2005).
5. Zheng Liu, "Between Business and Morality: Cultural Politics of Independent Bookshops in China," *Journal of Cultural Economy* 13, no. 4 (2020): 461–74.

6. Karl-Dieter Opp, "Grievances and Participation in Social Movements," *American Sociological Review* 53, no. 6 (1988): 853–64.
7. NPPA, *2014 Nian Quanguo Xinwen Chubanye Jiben Qingkuang* (*National Press and Publishing Report 2014*) (NPPA, 2015).
8. Hanci Chen, "250 Yi Jiaofu Dangao Liyi Lian Jiemi: Maishu Ru Maiyao," *Diyi Caijing* [China business news], May 16, 2012, http://m.yicai.com/news/1727018.html.
9. Miller, *Reluctant Capitalists*, 128.
10. Miller, *Reluctant Capitalists*, 129.
11. Miller, *Reluctant Capitalists*, 128.
12. Laura J. Miller, "Shopping for Community: The Transformation of the Bookstore into a Vital Community Institution," *Media, Culture & Society* 21, no. 3 (1999): 398.
13. *Xiaozi*, commonly translated as "petite bourgeoisie," is a Chinese term describing a lifestyle of chasing Western culture and tastes, practiced by middle-class white-collar workers in urban China.
14. Thompson, *Merchants of Culture*, 32; Miller, *Reluctant Capitalists*, 92.
15. Miller, *Reluctant Capitalists*, 103.
16. Tim Coats, "Chained and Independent: British Bookselling—A Revolution Accomplished," *Logos* 14, no. 1 (2003): 38.
17. Miller, *Reluctant Capitalists*, 92.
18. Will Smale, "The Man Who Transformed Bookshop Chain Foyles," BBC News, March 16, 2015, http://www.bbc.co.uk/news/business-31814498.
19. Jinping Xi, "Xi Jinping Zai Shiba Jie Zhongyang Jiwei Erci Quanhui Shang Fabiao Zhongyao Jianghua" (speech at the Second Plenary Session of the 18th Central Commission for Discipline Inspection), January 22, 2013, http://cpc.people.com.cn/n/2013/0122/c64094-20289660.html.

5. THE ECONOMICS OF INDEPENDENT BOOKSELLING

1. Lei Pi, "Di Shijiu Ci Quanguo Guomin Yuedu Diaocha Jieguo Fabu," *Gongyi Shibao* [China philanthropy times], April 26, 2022, GYSB14.pdf at gongyishibao.com.

2. Lai Xu, "2005–2014, Woguo Tushu Dingjia Shinian Zoushi Da Jiemi," *Chuban Shangwu Zhoubao* [China publishing today], March 1, 2016, http://www.cptoday.cn/news/detail/917.
3. CAPP, *Di 12 Ci Quanmin Yuedu Diaocha Baogao* (CAPP, 2015).
4. Constantinos C. Markides, "To Diversify or Not to Diversify," *Harvard Business Review* 75, no. 6 (1997): 93–186.
5. Markides, "To Diversify or Not to Diversify," 94.
6. Jean Baudrillard, *The Consumer Society: Myths and Structures* (Sage, 2016).
7. iResearch, *Report on China's Brewed Coffee Industry* (iResearch, 2022).
8. OpenBook, *Annual Report on the Chinese Book Retailing Market (2024)* (OpenBook, 2025).
9. Deloitte, *White Paper on China's Freshly Brewed Coffee Industry* (Deloitte, 2022).
10. Baudrillard, *The Consumer Society*.
11. Sisyphe Bookstore, "About Us," https://www.sisyphe.com.cn/#in-about-us, accessed April 28, 2023.
12. Sisyphe Bookstore, "About Us."
13. The information about this parent company's sectorial affiliation has been altered to maintain data anonymity.
14. Some information about the bookstore presented in this section has been altered to maintain data anonymity.
15. CVSource, https://www.cvsource.com.cn/.
16. CVSource, "Xixifu Shudian Huode Nanjing Zijin Kechuang Tianshilun Zhuzi," https://wxm.cvsource.com.cn/event/index.html?id=diMhIilyIXZxaCEpJyQlJg&ticket=eyJhbGciOiJIUzI1NiIsInR5cCI6IkpXVCJ9.eyJzaGFyZUlkIjoxOTcoNTYsImV4cCI6MTc1MTQ0OTA3Nywic2hhcmVUeXBlIjoxNywic2hhcmVVc2VySWQiOiJjMDcoYjU0NDMyNDA0NmU0OWMxNjU4MmIwZWVhYjdlMSIsImpoaSI, accessed June 25, 2025.

BIBLIOGRAPHY

Alibaba. "Alibaba Jituan Gongbu 2021 Nian Sanyuefen Jidu Ji 2021 Cainian Yeji." https://ali-home.alibaba.com/document-1491839814327074816, accessed June 13, 2025.

Analysys. *2016 Nian Diyi Jidu Zhongguo B2C Shichang Tushu Chubanwu Pinlei Shichang Fen'e*. Analysys, 2016. https://www.analysys.cn/article/detail/1000089.

Baensch, Robert. *The Publishing Industry in China*. Routledge, 2017.

Barton, Dominic, Yougang Chen, and Amy Jin. *Mapping China's Middle Class*. McKinsey, 2013.

Baudrillard, Jean. *The Consumer Society: Myths and Structures*. Sage, 2016.

Bourdieu, Pierre. "Vive ls Crise! For Heterodoxy in Social Science." *Theory and Society* 17 (1988): 773–87.

Bourdieu, Pierre. *The Field of Cultural Production: Essays on Art and Literature*. Polity, 1993.

Bourdieu, Pierre. "The Forms of Capital." *Cultural Theory: An Anthology* 1 (2011): 81–93.

Bryman, Alan. *Social Research Methods*. 5th ed. Oxford University Press, 2012.

Cambridge English Dictionary. "Individuality." https://dictionary.cambridge.org/dictionary/english/individuality, accessed May 16, 2022.

CAPP. *Di 12 Ci Quanmin Yuedu Diaocha Baogao*. CAPP, 2015.

CBNData. *2021 Tushu Xiaofei Bannian Baogao*. CBNData, 2021.

Chen, Hanci. "250 Yi Jiaofu Dangao Liyi Lian Jiemi: Maishu Ru Maiyao." *Diyi Caijing* [China business news], May 16, 2012. http://m.yicai.com/news/1727018.html.

Clark, Duncan. *Alibaba: The House That Jack Ma Built*. Ecco, 2016.
Clark, Giles, and Angus Phillips. *Inside Book Publishing*. 6th ed. Routledge, 2019.
Coats, Tim. "Chained and Independent: British Bookselling—A Revolution Accomplished." *Logos* 14, no. 1 (2003): 38.
Croll, Elisabeth. *China's New Consumers: Social Development and Domestic Demand*. Routledge, 2006.
Cusumano, Michael A., Annabelle Gawer, and David B. Yoffie. *The Business of Platforms: Strategy in the Age of Digital Competition, Innovation, and Power*. Harper Business, 2019.
CVSource. https://www.cvsource.com.cn/.
CVSource. "Xixifu Shudian Huode Nanjing Zijin Kechuang Tianshilun Zhuzi." https://wxm.cvsource.com.cn/event/index.html?id=diMhIilyIXZxaCEpJyQlJg&ticket=eyJhbGciOiJIUzI1NiIsInR5cCI6IkpXVCJ9.eyJzaGFyZU1kIjoxOTcoNTYsImV4cCI6MTc1MTQ0OTA3Nywic2hhcmVVeXBlIjoxNywic2hhcmVVc2VySWQiOiJjMDcoYjUoNDMyNDAoNmUoOWMxNjU4MmIwZWVhYjdjMlMSIsImpoaSI. Accessed June 25, 2025.
Deloitte. *White Paper on China's Freshly Brewed Coffee Industry*. Deloitte, 2022.
DeLisle, Jacques, Avery Goldstein, and Guobin Yang, eds. *The Internet, Social Media, and a Changing China*. University of Pennsylvania Press, 2016.
Des Forges, Alexander. "Burning with Reverence: The Economics and Aesthetics of Words in Qing (1644–1911) China." *PMLA/Publications of the Modern Language Association of America* 121, no. 1 (2006): 139–55.
Elder-Vass, Dave. *The Reality of Social Construction*. Cambridge University Press, 2012.
Farrell, Diana, Eric Beinhocker, Ulrich Gersch, Ezra Greenberg, Elizabeth Stephenson, Jonathan Ablett et al. *From 'Made in China' to 'Sold in China': The Rise of the Chinese Urban Consumer*. McKinsey, 2006.
iResearch. *Report on China's Brewed Coffee Industry*. iResearch, 2022.
Jinyuan Investment Group and Hurun Report. *2018 Zhongguo Xinzhongchan Quanceng Baipishu (Hurun 2018 China New Middle Class Report)*. https://res.hurun.cn/file/20190910/20190910143413817628.pdf, accessed June 13, 2025.
Kharas, Homi, and Meagan Dooley. *China's Influence on the Global Middle Class*. Brookings Institution, 2020.

Kim, Aimee, Lan Luan, and Daniel Zipser. *The Chinese Luxury Consumer*. McKinsey, 2019.

Kuang, Wenbo. "Feichang Shiqi De Wangmin Xingwei Tezheng." *Guoji Xinwenjie* [Journal of international communication], no. 5 (2003): 24–27.

Lee, Chin-Chuan. "Rethinking Political Economy: Implications for Media and Democracy in Greater China." *Javnost—the Public* 8, no. 4 (2001): 81–102.

Lenin, Vladimir I. *The State and Revolution*. International Publishers, 1968.

Liu, Zheng. "Between Business and Morality: Cultural Politics of Independent Bookshops in China." *Journal of Cultural Economy* 13, no. 4 (2020): 461–74.

Luhmann, Niklas. *The Making of Meaning: From the Individual to Social Order: Selections from Niklas Luhmann's Works on Semantics and Social Structure*. Ed. Christian Morgner, trans. Margaret Hiley, Christian Morgner, and Michael King. Oxford University Press, 2022.

Ma, Eric Kit-wai. "Rethinking Media Studies: The Case of China." In *De-Westernizing Media Studies*, ed. James Curran and Myung-Jin Park. Routledge, 2005.

Maguire, Jennifer S., and Hu Dan. "Not a Simple Coffee Shop: Local, Global and Glocal Dimensions of the Consumption of Starbucks in China." *Social Identities* 19, no. 5 (2013): 670–84.

Markides, Constantinos C. "To Diversify or Not to Diversify." *Harvard Business Review* 75, no. 6 (1997): 93–186.

Miller, Laura J. *Reluctant Capitalists: Bookselling and the Culture of Consumption*. University of Chicago Press, 2006.

Miller, Laura J. "Shopping for Community: The Transformation of the Bookstore into a Vital Community Institution." *Media, Culture & Society* 21, no. 3 (1999): 398.

NPPA. *1999 Nian Quanguo Xinwen Chubanye Jiben Qingkuang (National Press and Publishing Report 1999)*. NPPA, 2000.

NPPA. *2014 Nian Quanguo Xinwen Chubanye Jiben Qingkuang (National Press and Publishing Report 2014)*. NPPA, 2015.

NPPA. *2019 Nian Quanguo Xinwen Chubanye Jiben Qingkuang (National Press and Publishing Report 2019)*. NPPA, 2020.

OpenBook. *Annual Report on the Chinese Book Retailing Market (2016)*. OpenBook, 2017.

OpenBook. *Annual Report on the Chinese Book Retailing Market (2019)*. OpenBook, 2020.

OpenBook, *Annual Report on the Chinese Book Retailing Market (2022)*. OpenBook, 2023.

OpenBook, *Annual Report on the Chinese Book Retailing Market (2024)*. OpenBook, 2025.

Opp, Karl-Dieter. "Grievances and Participation in Social Movements." *American Sociological Review* 53, no. 6 (1988): 853–64.

Pi, Lei. "Di Shijiu Ci Quanguo Guomin Yuedu Diaocha Jieguo Fabu." *Gongyi Shibao* [China philanthropy times], April 26, 2022. GYSB14.pdf at gongyishibao.com.

Qiannan Wu, "Dangdang 2014 Nian Jing Lirun 8812 Wanyuan Tongbi Niukui," *Fenghuang Keji*, March 31 2015, https://tech.ifeng.com/a/20150331/41032082_0.shtml.

Repnikova, Maria. *Media Politics in China: Improvising Power Under Authoritarianism*. Cambridge University Press, 2017.

Sisyphe Bookstore. "About Us." https://www.sisyphe.com.cn/#in-about-us. Accessed April 28, 2023.

Smale, Will. "The Man Who Transformed Bookshop Chain Foyles." *BBC News*, March 16, 2015. http://www.bbc.co.uk/news/business-31814498.

Sun, Qingguo. "Economics of the Chinese Book Market." *Publishing Research Quarterly* 18, no. 3 (2003): 54–63.

Thompson, John B. *Books in the Digital Age: The Transformation of Academic and Higher Education Publishing in Britain and the United States* (Polity, 2005).

Thompson, John B. *Merchants of Culture: The Publishing Business in the Twenty-First Century*. Polity, 2010.

"Tushu Fenxiao Xin Shengtai: Geju Yu Qushi." *China Publishing Today*, June 8, 2016. https://www.jxxhsd.com/read_txt.asp?type=12&id=3452.

Veblen, Thorstein. *The Theory of the Leisure Class*. Houghton Mifflin, 1899 [1973].

Wen, Ting. "Dangdang Wang Er Jidu Jingli 2880 Wan, Chuang Lishi Xingao." *Shanghai Securities News*, August 15, 2014. https://paper.cnstock.com/html/2014-08/15/content_434834.htm.

Xi, Jinping. "Xi Jinping Zai Shiba Jie Zhongyang Jiwei Erci Quanhui Shang Fabiao Zhongyao Jianghua" (speech at the Second Plenary Session of the 18th Central Commission for Discipline Inspection), January 22, 2013. http://cpc.people.com.cn/n/2013/0122/c64094-20289660.html.

Xin, Guangwei. *Publishing in China: An Essential Guide.* 2nd ed. Cengage Learning, 2010.

Xu, Lai. "2005–2014, Woguo Tushu Dingjia Shinian Zoushi Da Jiemi." *Chuban Shangwu Zhoubao* [China publishing today], March 1, 2016. http://www.cptoday.cn/news/detail/917.

Xu, Yuanchong. "Congxin Suoyu Erbu Yueju—Tan Shici Fanyi Yu Zhongguo Wenhua Meng." *Guangming Daily*, April 28, 2015. https://epaper.gmw.cn/gmrb/html/2015-04/28/nw.D110000gmrb_20150428_1-11.htm.

Xun, Lu. "Men Wai Wen Tan." *Shen Bao* (August 24–September 10, 1934).

Yang, Deyan. "The Reform of the Book Distribution Industry and the Development of Non-State-Owned Bookstores in China." *Publishing Research Quarterly* 18, no. 2 (2002): 50–55.

Yu, Min, et al. "Zhongguo Minying Shuye Fazhan Yanjiu Baogao." *Chuban Faxing Yanjiu* [Publishing research], 11 (2003): 5–21.

Yu, Yang. "Sanfen Zhiyi Tushu Zhixiao, Tamen Douqu Na'er Le?" [One-third of published books are left unsold. Where have they gone to?], *Chuban Ren* [China publishers] 12 (2017): 32–36.

Yun, Qidong. "State Versus Market: A Perspective on China's Publishing Industry." *Logos* 24, no. 1 (2013): 19–29, https://doi.org/10.1163/1878-4712-11112009.

Zhang, Pan. "Tushu Wangshou Shichang: Dangdang, Jingdong, Amazon Sanfen Tianxia De Xi Yu You." *Zhongguo Chuban Chuanmei Shangbao* [China publishing & media journal], October 30, 2014, 14.

Zhang, Xiaosong, and Jichai Zhu. "Xi Jinping tan Wenchuang Chanye: Shouzheng Chuangxin, Jianchi Zhengque Daoxiang." *Xinhua Shidian*, September 18, 2020. http://politics.people.com.cn/n1/2020/0918/c1024-31866673.html.

Zhao, Heng. *Quan Xue Shi*, year unknown.

Zhao, Yuezhi. *Communication in China: Political Economy, Power, and Conflict.* Rowman & Littlefield, 2008.

INDEX

academic books, 40, 122–23, 160, 187, 221n13
academic book wholesaler, 160
academic monographs, 28, 122–23, 160, 161, 221n13
acquisitions, 33
aesthetics, 101, 102, 129, 130, 143, 146, 181; functionality and, 46, 84, 108–9; value of, 133, 175
affluence, 95, 108, 112
Alibaba Group (e-commerce platform), 52, 54, 56
altruism, in bookselling, 118–19
Amazon China, 53, 55
Amazon.com (e-commerce platform), 52–53, 142
angel investments, 208
Animal Farm (Orwell), 123, 126
applicant entity (*zhuban danwei*) (主办单位), 217
artifacts: cultural, 103, 121; decorative, 145, 152, 155; handmade, *185*, 186; historical, 98; intellectual, 121;

"Put power in a cage," 152, *153*, 154–55
atmosphere, 87, 144; cultural, 141; homelike, 145; political, 90, 129, 130, 156; in store decor, 90, 129–30, 141, 145–46, 150, 156
authoritarianism, 127
autographing parties, 134–35
autonomous region (*zizhi qu*) (自治区), 217
autonomy, 71, 74, 82, 110, 191, 212; in book retailing, 17; cultural, 14, 64, 68, 209; freedom and, 66, 72; intellectual, 5; loss of, 69; operational, 4, 13, 64–65; of personal bookstores, 62

Baensch, Robert, 6
Baudrillard, Jean, 175
Beijing Book Fairs, 16, 57
book booths, 47, 48
book company (*tushu gongsi*) (图书公司), 23, 217

book culture, 2, 6, 17–19, 21, 60; evolution of, 212; narratives that challenge, 12–14
book curation, 10, 210–11, 214; popular books and, 131–34; scholarly books and, 120–31; stocking and, 116–20
book distribution, 34–41, 123, 132, 158–59
book industry, 3–5, 19–22, 56, 60, 88, 209–10; conferences in, 1, 16; *Logos* on, 6; submarkets within, 132
book number allocation method, 31, 32
book number sale (*shuhao maimai*) (书号买卖), 23, 29–32, 217
book placement, 119–20
book prices, 164; changes in, *170*; consumers and, *170*, 172–73; median, 56, 105, 167, 169, 186; rising of, 56, 168–73, 187
book publishing (publishing house), 43, 122, 123, 220n7; book wholesalers, 32–34, 37, 38–41, 56, 158–65, 172, 205; categories of, 28–29, 122–23; central-level, 25–26, 27, 217; collaboration models in, 32–33; collaborative, 29–30, 31, 39, 217; English-speaking world of, 27–28; medium-sized, 162, 171; privately owned, 4, 29–30, 31–34, 39–42, 210; regional-level, 25, 26, 31, 217; state-owned, 22–30, 31–33, *37*, 40, 87, 161–62

book reading (*dushu*), 95
book retailing, 41–42, 132; autonomy in, 17; coffee shop market and, 181, *182*; commercialism in, 7, 11, 49; competitive advantage in, 2, 12, 17, 62, 86, 115, 175; cultural values in, 51; industry, 34, 54, 56; large, *37*; Miller on, 6–7; online, 34, 51–56, 142, 171–72, 212; physical, 61; small, *37*, 39. *See also* privately owned bookstores; Xinhua Bookstore
books: academic, 40, 122–23, 160, 187, 221n13; academic monographs, 28, 122–23, 160, 161, 221n13; for children, 106, 123, 124, 125, 160, 199, 204; complimentary copies of, 31–32, 137; general interest, 28, 34, 40, 122, 123, 129; popular, 131–34; scholarly, 48, 120–31; social science, 123, 160
book sales, 21; catering services influencing, 179; cultural events to boost, 135–36; high demand of, 47–48; for Xinhua Bookstore, 43, 44
book selection, 5, 64, 67, 81, 88, 96; cultural significance of, 117, 119; displays and, 129; effective, 116–18; factors in, 120–21; Miller on, 120–21; moral positioning and, 139, 211; online bookstores stocking and, 164; political framing in, 131; scholarly books and, 122, 124, 126–27; thematic categorization and, 129

bookselling, 1, 2–3; altruism in, 118–19; conundrum of, 21, 157–58; core business of, 5, 173, 174, 213; cultural significance of, 94–96, 97–98; culture of, 8–14, 62–63; *jingxi zizhi* tradition and, 98–99; moral ramifications of, 94; part-time, 199–202; quasi-educators in, 92–93; scholarly books and, 123–24

bookstore owner, 76, 81, 85, 162–63, 188; educational vision of, 92–93; as guardians of cultural values, 8; nonstate, 80, 84, 202; part-time bookselling of, 199–202; personal imprint of, 77, 82, 126–27, 154; political framing of, 10, 13, 14, 90; on stocking, 158, 165; structures for, 61–62, 64–75, 179; WeChat group for, 59

bookstore-run coffee shop, 91, 144, 175–83, 194

bookstores: Amazon dominance over, 52; brick-and-mortar, 1, 34, 44, 50, 55, 134, 142; chain, 48, 61–63, 76, 119, 135, 143–44; coffee shop in, 91, 144, 175–83, 194; co-owners of, 200; cultural events at, 10–11, 102, 134–41, 152, 175, 183; displays at, 119–20, 128–30, 147, 150, 152, 154, 156, 199; financial burdens of, 188, 190; mall-based, 61, 139, 143, 188–89, 191–92; nonindependent, 2, 4, 15–16, 81, 102, 104–6, 121; O₂Sun Bookstore, 145–46; ownership structure of, 14, 61–62, 64–75, 80, 84, 179, 202; personal, 61–62; rent of, 21, 44, 139, 166, 188–93, 195, 198–99, 201, 205; scholarly, 48–49, 57–58; Sisyphe Bookstore, 193, *194*, 195–98, 208; socialization at, 89–90, 92–93; value orientation of, 77; VC-backed, 65–66, 69–73. *See also* independent bookstore; privately owned bookstore; Xinhua Bookstore

book supply chain, 89

book wholesale centers (*tushu pifa shichang*), 16, 38–39, 41, 56, 132, 159–61

book wholesalers: academic, 160; for children, 160; distribution and, 32–33, 162–63, 172; local, 34, 38–41, 56, 158–65, 205; privately owned, 33, 37, 41; shop for, *38*

Bourdieu, Pierre, 18, 79; on consumption, 108–10; on cultural preferences, 109; on economic capital, 103, 107; Veblen and, 102–3

brick-and-mortar bookstores, 1, 34, 44, 50, 55, 134, 142

Bureau of Press and Publication, 24–25

burning paper, 96, 97, 98

capital, 198, 203; distribution of, 105, 107; economic, 103, 104, 105, 106, 107, 186; gains, 66; symbolic, 104–5, 106–7; venture, 65–66, 68–75, 206–8

capital operation, 66, 199, 222n4
CAPP. *See* Chinese Academy of Press and Publication
carnivalesque events, 135
categories, of book publishing, 28–29
catering services, 175, 177, 179
CCP. *See* Chinese Communist Party
Central Commission for Discipline Inspection, 152, 225n19
central-level publishing house (*zhongyang ji chuban she*) (中央级出版社), 25–26, 27, 217
chain bookstores, 48, 61–63, 76, 119, 135, 143–44
Chaoyang District, 78
children's books, 106, 123, 124, 125, 160, 199, 204
China. *See specific topics*
China Post system, 35
China Publishing Group (CPG), 27
China Publishing Today (trade journal), 169
China Resources (real estate developer), 195
China South CS-Booky Cultural Media Co Ltd., 33
China South Publishing & Media Group, 27, 33
China Standard Book Numbers (CSBN), 23, 29–33, 220n2
China tea set, *185*
Chinese Academy of Press and Publication (CAPP), 168, 169–70
Chinese Communist Party (CCP), 25–26, 42

Chuban Guanli Tiaoli (Regulations on Publication Administration) (出版管理条例), 23, 24–25, 87, 217
chuban she (publishing house) (出版社). *See* book publishing
Chubanwu shichang guanli guiding (Provisions on the Administration of the Publication Market) (出版物市场管理规定), 87, 217
Clark, Giles, 6
class-based explanations, 112, 114
class positions, 108–10
Coats, Tim, 143
coffee market, 112, 180, 181
coffee prices, 179, *180*
coffee shop, bookstore-run, 91, 144, 175–83, 194
coffee shop market, 179, 181, *182*
collaborative book publishing, 29–30, 31, 39, 217
collaborative publishing (*hezuo chuban*) (合作出版), 29–30, 31, 39, 217
commercialism, 63, 66, 72, 79–80, 118, 121; attitudes towards, 18, 198; in book retailing, 7, 11, 49; commercialization and, 75, 198; cultural values and, 8, 63; embracing, 156, 192, 196, 198; forces of, 60, 75, 156, 197; independent bookstores and, 18, 78, 125, 209; nonbook merchandise and, 187; of Sisyphe Bookstore, 195–98; study aid

books and, 49; titles and, 164, 175, 187
commercialization, 75, 79, 156, 157, 196, 198
community-bonding, at cultural events, 136, 137
competitive advantage: in book retailing, 2, 12, 17, 62, 86, 115, 175; cultural distinguishing and, 102; cultural profile and, 175; of Xinhua Bookstore, 44
complimentary copies, of books, 31–32, 137
computer, communication, and consumer electronics ($_3$C), 53–54
conferences, book industry, 1, 16
Confucian classics, 95, 96–97
consignment contracts, 161–62
conspicuous consumption, 11, 108, 109–14, 175
constitutionalism (宪政), 129, *130*
consumer price index (CPI), 169, *170*
consumers, 6–7, 38, 46, 53–54, 56, 102; attracting, 192–93; book prices and, *170*, 172–73; demands of, 213; income of, 180; influence over, 128–29; middle-class, 109, 112, 113–14; online, 52; preferences of, 182–83; sign value and, 175, 186; at Sisyphe Bookstore, 196–98
consumption: Bourdieu on, 108–10; choices of, 108, 110; conspicuous, 11, 108, 109–14, 175; cultural distinguishing and, 101; cultural goods, 9, 24, 79, 87, 103, 107; cultural production and, 2

controversial authors, 10, 89, 91, 140
conundrum of bookselling, 21, 157–58
co-owners, of bookstores, 200
core business, of bookselling, 5, 173, 174, 213
corporate ownership, 65, 66
corporatization reform, 26, 28–29, 74, 171
COVID-19 pandemic, 54, 206, 213
CPG. *See* China Publishing Group
CPI. *See* consumer price index
CSBN. *See* China Standard Book Numbers
CS-Booky (privately owned publishing house), 33
cultural artifacts, 103, 121
cultural atmosphere, 141
cultural autonomy, 14, 64, 68, 209
cultural commitments, 63, 65–66, 118, 157, 187, 191, 198
cultural discernment, 111
cultural distinguishing, 101; competitive advantage and, 102; moral positioning and, 9, 11, 17, 18, 20, 86, 115, 156, 209; strategy of, 10, 103, 105, 107, 114, 141, 211
cultural elitism, 133–34
cultural enterprises, 8, 9, 115, 157, 211–12
cultural events, 10–11, 102, 134–41, 152, 175, 183
cultural experiences, 103, 108, 111, 114, 142, 182; through cultural events, 10–11, 102, 134, 152, 175, 183; interior design enhancing, 102, 146, 148

cultural goals, 66–67, 78, 191
cultural goods, 9, 24, 79, 87, 103, 107
cultural industry, 5, 87, 204
cultural institutions, 8–9, 103–5, 209
cultural logic, 103–4
culturally adapted strategies, 9, 11–12, 17–18, 20–21, 86, 115. *See also* cultural distinguishing; moral positioning; political framing
cultural preferences, 109
cultural production, 11, 17, 18–19, 21, 75; consumption and, 2; cultural values and, 74, 104, 151, 156, 157; English-language literature and, 12; field of, 209–10; mode of, 79; political influence over, 87–88
cultural profile, 175
cultural significance: of book selection, 117, 119; of bookselling, 94–96, 97–98
cultural sociology, 6, 19
cultural standards, 79–80, 106, 125, 133, 193, 196
cultural taste, 11, 108, 111–12, 141
cultural values, 117, 209; in book retailing, 51; bookstore owner as guardians of, 8; commercialism and, 8, 63; cultural production and, 74, 104, 151, 156, 157; economic considerations and, 11, 120; hierarchy of tastes and, 108–10; independent identity and, 63; profits and, 51, 78, 107, 125
cultural visions, 115, 157
CVSource (VC database), 207, 208

Dangdang.com (book retailing website), 51–55, 164, 171
decline, of local book wholesalers, 158–61
decorative artifacts, 145, 152, 155
Deloitte report, 182
democracy (民主), 129, *130*
Des Forges, Alexander, 96, 97
difang ji chuban she (regional-level publishing house) (地方级出版社), 25, 26, 31, 217
digital age, 2, 88, 111, 142, 212–15
direct book number sales, 30, 31, 32
Discipline and Punish (Foucault), 123
discount rates, 40
discounts, 55–56, 105, 171–73
displays, 147, 150, 152, 154, 156, 199; arrangements for, 119–20, 128; book selection and, 129; strategy for, 130
disposable income, 113, 169, *170*, *180*
distinctions, 83, 141, 209; class-based, 112; cultural, 68, 101, 102, 107, 114, 134, 151, 186, 203; social, 111; theory of, 108
distribution: book, 34–41, 123, 132, 158–59; of capital, 105, 107; outsourcing, 161; wholesalers and, 32–33, 162–63, 172
diversification, 194, 213, 214; coffee shop for, 182–83; nonbook, 173–75, 187, 191, 207; strategy for, 185
Doast rituals, of paper burning, 96, 97, 98
dominant class, 108

duli (independent) (独立), 82–83
duli shudian (independent bookstore) (独立书店). *See* independent bookstore
dushu (book reading), 95
dushu ren (people who read books), 95
dynasty: Han, 82–83; Ming, 96; Qing, 97; Song, 95

e-commerce, 53–54, 56, 142, 212–13
economic capital, 103, 104, 105, 106, 107, 186
economic considerations, 7–8, 18, 21, 117–18, 125, 176; of cultural enterprises, 9; cultural values and, 11, 120; goals for, 10, 11, 13–14, 17, 90
economic dynamics, 157, 193
economic efficiency, 111
economic logic, 18, 103, 104, 110–11
educational book market, 29, 30, 43–44, 160
educational visions, 92–96, 101, 125
English-language literature, 12, 19, 22, 122, 123
English-speaking world, 7, 19, 27–28
equity stake, 69
er qudao (secondary channel) (二渠道), 35, 36, *37*, 39, 218
evolution, of book culture, 212
external investments, 65–66, 70, 198, 202–8

financial burdens, of bookstores, 188, 190
Foreign Language Bookstore (*waiwen shudian*) (外文书店), 218
Foucault, Michel, 123
Foyles (independent bookstore), 144
freedom (自由), 66, 72, 129, *130*
functionality, aesthetics and, 46, 84, 108–9

general interest books, 28, 34, 40, 122, 123, 129
gexing (individuality), 5, 80, 81
gift shop, 144, *184*
gross profit margins, 55, 105–6, 166
Guangzhou Province, 195
Guizhou Province, 193, 194–95

Han dynasty, poem from, 82–83
Hello, The Independent Bookstore (2011), 57, *58*
Hemingway, Ernest, 148
Henan Xinhua Bookstore Group, 42
hezuo chuban (collaborative publishing) (合作出版), 29–30, 31, 39, 217
hierarchy of tastes, 108–10
high culture, 8–9
historical artifacts, 98
homelike atmosphere, 145
Hugo, Victor, 147
Hugo Bookshop, *148*
Hurun 2018 China New Middle-Class Report, 113

idiosyncrasy, 77, 82
imperial examinations, 95, 96–97
incentives, 115, 188, 206
independence, 5, 68, 70, 76, 77, 82; challenge to, 65, 73–74, 197–98; cultural values and, 209; economic, 80; financial, 85; freedom and, 71, 72; parent companies and, 202; political, 80; profitability and, 190–91; question of, 78
independent (*duli*) (独立), 82–83
independent bookstore (*duli shudian*) (独立书店), *149*, *150*, 217; approaching, 3–8; China tea set sold in, *185*; coffee shop inside, *177*, *178*; commercialism and, 18, 78, 125, 209; conspicuous consumption and, 110–14; as cultural enterprises, 8, 9, 115, 157, 211–12; as cultural institutions, 8–9; cultural profile of, 175; cultural visions of, 115, 157; economic dynamics of, 157, 193; gift shop in, *144*, *184*; independent ethos and, 78, 80–85; investors and, 65–66; Miller on, 61, 63; as multifunctional cultural spaces, 206, 211, 214; noneconomic values of, 117–18; operational autonomy for, 4–5, 13, 64–65; operational strategies of, 75; owners or managers of, 2, 15, 58, 59, 64; qualitative research methods on, 14–17; revenue of, 21; rise of, 1–2, 17, 57–59; scholarly bookstores connection to, 49; uniqueness of, 76, 77, 82; in United States, 5, 60–64; venture capital investments influence on, 65, 68–69, 70–75, 206–8. *See also* independent identity; scholarly books; store decor
independent chain bookstores, 63
independent ethos, 78, 80–85
independent identity, 4, 5, 8, 14, 20, 59, 60; compromise of, 70, 71; corporate ownership and, 66; cultural values and, 63; multiple branches operations and, 76–79; organizational ownership tied to, 72, 73, 74; of personal bookstores, 62
individuality (*gexing*), 5, 80–84
influence: of moral positioning, 94, 96; over consumers, 128–29; political, 13, 18, 74, 87–89, 151, 156, 197; of social hierarchies, 104
Inside Book Publishing (Clark and Phillips), 6
intellectual artifacts, 121
interior design, 45–46, 102, 146, 148
internalist, 71
International Standard Book Number (ISBN), 220n2
interviews-based qualitative research, 14–17
inventory, 41, 159, 167, 169, 206; dissatisfaction with, 165; management of, 119, 195; naming of, 129; of nonbook merchandise,

125; selection of, 64, 116–20, 131; SKU for, 184; stocking, 39, 127; unsold, 163
investments, 182, 190, 191, 200; angel, 208; external, 65–66, 70, 198, 199, 202–8; nonbook corporations, 67, 203–5; venture capital, 65, 68–69, 70–75, 206–8
iResearch (market research firm), 181, *182*
ISBN. *See* International Standard Book Number

JD.com (e-commerce platform), 53, 54–56, 164, 171
Jiangsu Phoenix Publishing & Media Group, 27
jiaofushu (study aid books), 43
jingxi zizhi (respecting and cherishing written characters and paper) (敬惜字纸), 96–99
Jin Weizhu, 193–94, 195
Joyo.com (book retailing website), 51–52, 53

Lenin, Vladimir, 98
"liberation through reading" (slogan), 155–56
Librairie Avant-Garde (independent bookstore), *147*
Liu Suli, 57–58
local book wholesalers, 34, 38–39, 41, 56; decline of, 158–61; stocking, 40, 159, 161–65
Logos (academic journal), 6
lower class, 108, 109

low profit margins, 68–69, 105, 166–67
Luhmann, Niklas, 83
Lu Xun, 98

main channel (*zhu qudao*) (主渠道), 35, *36*, 39, 158–59, 218
mainstream culture, 88, 151
mall-based bookstores, 61, 139, 143, 188–89, 191–92
management roles: for independent bookstore, 2, 15, 58, 59, 64; VC and, 69
Markides, Constantinos, 173–74
MAXQDA (data analysis software), 16
McKinsey report (2013), 113
median household disposable income (MHDI), *180*
medium-sized publishing house, 162, 171
Merchants of Culture (Thompson), 6, 19
MHDI. *See* median household disposable income
middle-class consumer, 109, 112, 113–14
middle dealer (*zhongpan shang*) (中盘商), 37, 218
Miller, Laura J., 61–63, 72, 82, 93–94, 143; on autographing parties, 134–35; on book retailing, 6–7; on book selection, 120–21; *Reluctant Capitalists*, 6, 19; Thompson and, 7–8
Ming dynasty, 96

minimum order threshold, 163
Min Yu, 50
moralization, 101
moral positioning, 10, 91; book selection and, 139, 211; cultural distinguishing and, 9, 11, 17, 18, 20, 86, 115, 156, 209; on cultural events, 139–40; educational visions, 92–96, 101, 125; political framing and, 11; respectful visions, 96–100, 101, 125; scholarly books and, 125–26
moral visions, 101, 139–40; educational, 92–96; respectful, 96–100
multifunctional cultural spaces, 206, 211, 214
multiple branches, of operation, 75–76, 77, 78–79, 80, 187
municipal head store (*shidian*) (市店), 35, 36, 40, 218
municipalities (*zhixia shi*) (直辖市), 217

National Press and Publication Administration (NPPA) (*xinwen chuban shu*) (新闻出版署), 23, 24–25, 30–31, 55, 217
New York Stock Exchange (NYSE), 52
1984 (Orwell), 123, 126
nonbook businesses, 21, 68; diversification of, 173–75, 187, 191, 207; in-store coffee shop, 91, 144, 175–83
nonbook corporations, 67, 202–6

nonbook merchandise, 68, 118–19, 125, 156, 183–87, 192, 197, 214
nonconformity, 5, 85
noncorporate ownership, 63
noneconomic values, 117–18
nonindependent bookstores, 2, 4, 15–16, 81, 102, 104–6, 121
nonstate-owned media, 12–13, 18–19
no-return, no-exchange policy, 163
NPPA. *See* National Press and Publication Administration
NYSE. *See* New York Stock Exchange

O$_2$Sun Bookstore, 145–46
one book one number (*yishu yihao*) (一书一号), 31, 217
online book retailing, 34, 51–56, 142, 171–72, 212
online bookstores, 37, 194; competition from, 167–68; large, 39, 40, 41–42, 101, 164; physical bookstores and, 1–2, 55; stocking and, 164–65; Tmall Books, 53–54, 56, 164
OpenBook data, 51, 55, 56
operational autonomy, 4, 13, 64–65
operations: independence and, 75; multiple branches of, 75–76, 77, 78–79, 80, 187; single-store, 75–76, 78, 214
Orwell, George, 123, 126
ownership structure, of bookstores, 14, 61–62, 64–75, 80, 84, 179, 202

parent company, 26, 66–68, 70, 198, 202–4, 226n13
part-time bookselling, 199–202
payment arrangements, 40–41
People's Republic of China, 220n1
people who read books (*dushu ren*), 95
personal bookstores, 61–62
personal imprint, of bookstore owner, 77, 82, 126–27, 154
petite bourgeoisie (*xiaozi*), 140, 225n13
Phillips, Angus, 6
physical bookstores, 111, 156, 205–6; online bookstores and, 1–2, 55; store decor in, 142–44
political atmosphere, 90, 129, 130, 156
political framing, 9, 18–19, 86–89; in book selection, 131; of bookstore owner, 10, 13, 14, 90; cultural events and, 140–41; moral positioning and, 11; scholarly books and, 126–31; socio-political effect of, 90–91; store decor and, 90, 151–56
political influence, 13, 18, 74, 87–88, 151, 156, 197
popular books, 131–34
power (权力), 152, 154–55
price wars, 55, 100
printed books, 132, 168, 171
print runs, 171
private book distributors, 35, 38
privately owned bookstores, 40–42, 44, 46, 47–48, 64, 132; conventional, 57; fall of, 49, 50, 51; nonindependent, 4, 51, 84, 105, 146, 150, 151; stock for, 39, 158–59; traditional, 145
privately owned book wholesalers, 33, 37, 41
privately owned publishing companies, 4, 29–30, 34, 39–42, 210; complimentary copies of books from, 31–32; CS-Booky, 33; secondary channels of, 37; state-owned publishing houses acquisitions of, 33
profitability, 121; achieving, 66, 67, 131, 166, 207–8; of coffee shops, 179–83; cultural values and, 51, 78, 107, 125; discounts and, 39; independence and, 190–91; nonbook merchandise and, 185–86; noneconomic values and, 117–18; of scholarly books, 124; of shopping malls, 189–91; stocking and, 158; struggles with, 165–73
profit margins, 124–25; gross, 55, 105–6, 166; low, 68–69, 105, 166–67
Protestant Ethic and the Spirit of Capitalism, The (Weber), 123
province (*sheng*) (省), 217
provincial head store (*shengdian*) (省店), 35, 36, 40, 218
Provisions on the Administration of the Publication Market (*Chubanwu shichang guanli guiding*) (出版物市场管 理规定), 87, 217

public service organisation (*shiye danwei*) (事业单位), 26, 46, 47, 218
publishing groups, 33; China South Publishing & Media Group, 27; Jiangsu Phoenix Publishing & Media Group, 27; provincial, 26, 42; regional, 26–27; Shanghai Century Publishing Group, 26–27
publishing house (*chuban she*) (出版社). *See* book publishing
Publishing in China (Xin), 6
publishing industry, 6, 122, 123, 169, 220n7; global players in, 27; minimum order threshold imposed by, 163; the state controlling, 88–89; stocking and, 161–63. *See also* book publishing
Publishing Industry in China, The (Baensch), 6
publishing process, 27
Publishing Research Quarterly (academic journal), 6
publishing studies, 6, 19
"Put power in a cage," 152, *153*, 154–55

Qing dynasty, 97
Qingguo Sun, 48
quasi-educators, in bookselling, 92–93

real estate, 55, 103, 189, 200, 202, 203; China Resources, 195; developers of, 188; of shopping malls, 191, 194; Sisyphe Bookstore, 193; Xinhua Bookstore, 44
recommended retail prices (RRP), 167, 171
reduction, of rent, 21, 188, 190–93, 198
regional-level publishing house (*difang ji chuban she*) (地方级出版社), 25, 26, 31, 217
Regulations on Publication Administration (Chuban Guangli Tiaoli), 23, 24–25, 87, 217
Reluctant Capitalists (Miller), 6, 19
rent, of bookstores, 139, 189, 199, 201, 205; high, 44, 166, 188, 190; reduction of, 21, 188, 190–93, 198; waiving agreements for, 195
respectful visions, 96–100, 101, 125
respecting and cherishing written characters and paper (*jingxi zizhi*) (敬惜字纸), 96–99
responsible editor (*zeren bianji*) (责任编辑), 218
retail branches, of Xinhua Bookstore, *36*, 64
returns, 8, 191–92, 203, 208; economic, 79, 107, 117; long-term, 68
revenue: from cultural events, 138–39; of independent bookstores, 21, 166–67; nonbook merchandise generating, 68, 118–19, 125, 156, 184, 192, 197, 214; scissors effect and, 188; of Xinhua Bookstores, 44–45

Roaming Guide to Chinese Independent Bookstores, A (2013), 57, 58, 59
RRP. *See* recommended retail prices

sales volumes: high, 106; low, 167
sanshen zhi (three-step examination) (三审制), 31, 217, 220n7
SARS. *See* severe acute respiratory syndrome
scholarly books (*xueshu shu*), 48; book selection and, 122, 124, 126–27; bookselling and, 123–24; moral positioning and, 125–26; political framing and, 126–31; prioritization of, 120–25; profitability of, 124; symbolic power of, 128, 130–31
scholarly bookstores (*xueshu shudian*), 48–49, 57–58
scissors effect, 188
secondary channel (*er qudao*) (二渠道), 35, 36, 37, 39, 218
severe acute respiratory syndrome (SARS), 51–52
Shandong Xinhua Bookstore Group, 42
Shanghai Century Publishing Group, 26–27
Shanghai Municipal Government, 26–27
shares and stocks, 33, 103, 207–8
sheng (province) (省), 217
shengdian (provincial head store) (省店), 35, 36, 40, 218

shidian (municipal head store) (市店), 35, 36, 40, 218
shiye danwei (public service organisation) (事业单位), 26, 46, 47, 218
shopping malls, 192, 194, 195, 197, 203; courting between, 189; profitability of, 189–91; rent reduction and, 21, 188, 191
shuhao maimai (book number sale) (书号买卖), 23, 29–30, 31–32, 217
Sichuan Xinhua Winshare Publishing and Media Group, 42
sign value, 175, 186
single-store operations, 75–76, 78, 214
Sisyphe Bookstore, 193–98, 208
1688.com (book retailing website), 52
SKU. *See* stock keep unit
slogans, 90, 146–47, 152–56
socialization, at bookstores, 89–90, 92–93
social media, 2, 5, 17, 102, 207, 212
social participation, 89, 126–27, 131, 154
social science books, 123, 160
social significance, of books, 95–97
social status, 11, 95, 108, 109, 151
socio-economic conditions, 107, 108, 110, 111–12, 141
SOE. *See* state-owned enterprises
Song dynasty, 95
Starbucks, 180, 183
the state, 19; political influence of, 13, 18, 74, 87–88, 151, 156, 197; publishing industry

the state (*continued*)
controlled by, 88–89; sanctioned mainstream culture of, 88
State and Revolution, The (Lenin), 98
state-owned enterprises (SOE), 24, 25, 26, 64
state-owned publishing houses, 22–23, *24*, 25–30; book number allocation method and, 31, 32; consignment contracts with, 161–62; discounts given by, 40; privately owned publishing companies acquisitions of, 33; regulations over, 87; secondary channel of, *37*; shares and stocks in, 33. *See also* Xinhua Bookstore
stocking: book curation and, 116–20; bookstore owner on, 158, 165; for bookstores, 21, 34–35, 39, 40–41, 46, 125–28, 131–33; obtainability for, 165; online bookstores and, 164–65; for privately owned bookstores, 39; problems with, 158–63; publishing industry and, 161–63; shares and, 33, 103, 207–8; SKU, 184; strategy for, 131–32
stock keep unit (SKU) code, 184
store decor, 142–43; atmosphere created in, 90, 129–30, 141, 145–46, 150, 156; cultural distinguishing and, 145–51; political framing and, 90, 151–56; Western cultural elements in, 146–51

study aid books (*jiaofushu*), 43, 106, 107, 124, 125, 126; commercialism and, 49; as popular books, 132–33
subsidies, 21, 103, 201; from parent companies and external investors, 202–8; receiving, 198–99
supervising organ (*zhuguan jiguan*) (主管机关), 25, 26, 217
symbolic capital, 104–5, 106–7

Taobao.com (book retailing website), 52, 54
tea houses, 175, 176, 177
thematic categories, 128–29, 130
Thompson, John B., 6–7, 19, 119
$_3$C. *See* computer, communication, and consumer electronics
three-step examination (*sanshen zhi*) (三审制), 31, 217, 220n7
Tmall Books (e-commerce platform), 53–54, 56, 164
trade book publications, 7, 28, 57
tushu gongsi (book company) (图书公司), 23, 217
tushu pifa shichang (book wholesale centers), 16, 38–39, 41, 56, 132, 159–61

uniqueness, 76, 77, 82
United Kingdom (UK): book industry in, 19, 20, 60; Foyles in, 144; independent bookstores in, 61; publishing house in, 27; Starbucks in, *180*

United States (US): book industry in, 19, 20, 60; independent bookstore in, 5, 60–64; publishing house in, 27
unused book numbers, 30
upper class, 109

value-added tax (VAT), 45, 205
value orientation, of bookstore, 77
VAT. *See* value-added tax
VC. *See* venture capital
Veblen, Thorstein, 11, 102–3, 108–11
venture capital (VC): bookstores funded by, 65–66, 69–73; investments, 65, 68–69, 70–75, 206–8; management roles and, 69
venture capitalists, 65–66, 68–69, 73, 206
voluntary acceptance, 71
vouching mechanisms, 162

waiving agreements, 195
waiwen shudian (Foreign Language Bookstore) (外文书店), 218
waste, 110–11
Weber, Max, 123
WeChat (group messaging app), 16–17, 59, 206, 213, 214
Western cultural elements, in store decor, 146–51
Wilde, Oscar, 148

xiaozi (petite bourgeoisie), 140, 225n13
Xi Jinping, 74, 152, 225n19

Xin, Guangwei, 6
Xinhua Bookstore (*xinhua shudian*) (新华书店), 4, 10, 33, 34, 41, 42; book sales, *43*, *44*; competitive advantage of, 44; cultural commitments, 63, 65–66, 118, 157, 187, 191, 198; discounts offered by, 40; interior design of, 45–46; lack of individuality in, 83–84; main channel for, *36*; municipal head store for, 35, *36*, 40, 218; popular books in, 132; provincial head store for, 35, *36*, 40, 218; redecorated, *47*; reliability of, 162–63; retail branches of, *36*, 64; revenue of, 44–45
xinhua shudian (Xinhua Bookstore) (新华书店), 218
xinwen chuban shu (National Press and Publication Administration) (新闻出版署), 23, 24–25, 217
xueshu shu (scholarly books), 48
xueshu shudian (scholarly bookstores), 48–49

yishu yihao (one book one number) (一书一号), 31, 217

zeren bianji (responsible editor) (责任编辑), 218
zhixia shi (municipalities) (直辖市), 217
zhongpan shang (middle dealer) (中盘商), 37, 218

zhongyang ji chuban she (central-level publishing house) (中央级出版社), 25–26, 27, 217

zhuban danwei (applicant entity) (主办单位), 217

zhuguan jiguan (supervising organ) (主管机关), 25, 26, 217

zhu qudao (main channel) (主渠道), 35, 36, 39, 158–59, 218

zizhi qu (autonomous region) (自治区), 217

GPSR Authorized Representative: Easy Access System Europe, Mustamäe tee 50, 10621 Tallinn, Estonia, gpsr.requests@easproject.com

www.ingramcontent.com/pod-product-compliance
Lightning Source LLC
Chambersburg PA
CBHW032336300426
44109CB00041B/1003